A Beginner's Guide to Kiln-Formed Glass

Fused, Slumped, Cast

A Beginner's Guide to Kiln-Formed Glass

Fused, Slumped, Cast

BRENDA GRIFFITH

LARK BOOKS

A Division of Sterling Publishing Co., Inc.
New York / London

Editor: Chris Rich
Senior Editor: Suzanne J. E. Tourtillott
Art Director: Megan Kirby
Cover Designer: Cindy LaBreacht
Assistant Editor: Shannon P. Quinn-Tucker
Associate Art Director: Travis Medford
Art Production Assistant: Jeff Hamilton
Editorial Assistance: Dawn Dillingham, Cassie Moore
Art Intern: Michael Foreman
Illustrator: Bernadette Wolf
Photographer: John Widman

Notes about Suppliers

Usually, the supplies you need for making the projects in Lark books can be found at your local craft supply store, discount mart, home improvement center, or retail shop relevant to the topic of the book. Occasionally, however, you may need to buy materials or tools from specialty suppliers. In order to provide you with the most up-to-date information, we have created a listing of suppliers on our web site, which we update on a regular basis. Visit us at www.larkbooks.com, click on "Craft Supply Sources," and then click on the relevant topic. You will find numerous companies listed with their web address and/or mailing address and phone number.

Photo at right
Brenda Griffith
Coptic Blue Eye Box, 2006
6 x 5½ x 3 inches (15.2 x14x 7.6 cm)
Bullseye glass; fused and raked; cut and full-standing fused
Photo by Bart Kasten

Library of Congress Cataloging-in Publication Data

Griffith, Brenda, 1961
   A Beginner's Guide to Kiln-Formed Glass : Fused, Slumped, Cast / Brenda Griffith. --
1st ed.
      p.   cm.
   Includes index.
   ISBN-13: 978-1-57990-909-3
   ISBN-10 1-57990-909-4

10 9 8 7 6 5 4 3 2

First Edition

Published by Lark Books, A Division of
Sterling Publishing Co., Inc.
387 Park Avenue South, New York, N.Y. 10016

Text © 2007, Brenda Griffith
Photography © 2007, Lark Books unless otherwise specified
Illustrations © 2007, Lark Books unless otherwise specified

Distributed in Canada by Sterling Publishing,
c/o Canadian Manda Group, 165 Dufferin Street
Toronto, Ontario, Canada M6K 3H6

Distributed in the United Kingdom by GMC Distribution Services,
Castle Place, 166 High Street, Lewes, East Sussex, England BN7 1XU

Distributed in Australia by Capricorn Link (Australia) Pty Ltd.,
P.O. Box 704, Windsor, NSW 2756 Australia

If you have questions or comments about this book, please contact:
Lark Books
67 Broadway
Asheville, NC 28801
(828) 253-0467

Manufactured in China

ISBN-13: 978-1-57990-909-3
ISBN-10 1-57990-909-4
For information about custom editions, special sales, premium and corporate purchases, please contact Sterling Special Sales Department at 800-805-5489 or specialsales@sterlingpub.com.

To Dave, the love of my life and partner of my days. You know everything you did to encourage and help me so I could write this book. More important, I know, too. Thank you. And to Jessie for understanding when Mommy had to write and couldn't read to her or play with her instead.

CONTENTS

Brenda Griffith
"Cosmos" Morceaux de Verre Panel, 2006
17 x 13 x 4 inches (43.2 x 33x 10.2 cm)
Bullseye glass; crushed, blended, fused
Photo by Bart Kasten

There's something magical about kiln forming glass. It's an art that transcends the mere assembly of pieces; glass transmutes into something entirely new with the application of intense heat and gravity. More than 20 years ago, I put my first pieces of glass in a cold kiln, heated them up, cooled them down again, and began my quest for the glass version of the Philosopher's Stone. Since then, my passion—in the pursuit of art—has been to observe, study, and learn all that I can about the nature of glass, heat, and gravity. The results are distilled in this book—*A Beginner's Guide to Kiln-Formed Glass.*

I wrote this book to engage and excite the beginner with easy-to-follow, step-by-step instructions, how-to photos, and illustrations that take the mystery out of the kiln-forming process. At the same time, I wanted to empower more experienced kiln formers by replacing the alchemy of kiln forming with the science behind it so that they could move from producing serendipitous accidents to consistently creating beautiful, planned works.

A Beginner's Guide to Kiln-Formed Glass opens with an overview of the art of kiln forming. This is followed by descriptions of

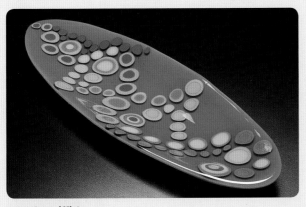

Brenda Griffith
Pop Art Sea Serpent, 2005
19 x 7 x 1 inches (48.3 x 17.8 x 2.5 cm)
Bullseye glass; fused, slumped
Photo by Bart Kasten

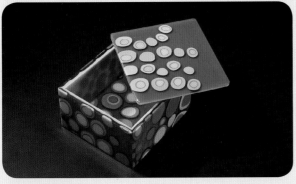

Brenda Griffith
Pop Art Grouper Box, 2006
6 x 5½ x 3 inches (15.2 x 14 x 7.6 cm)
Bullseye glass; fused, cut and full-standing fused
Photo by Bart Kasten

Brenda Griffith
Puzzle Bowl, 2006
12 x 3 inches 30.5 x 7.6 cm)
Bullseye glass; fused and slumped
Photo by Bart Kasten

the materials and tools used to prepare and kiln form glass. You don't need to purchase everything listed; you can get up and running with a very modest investment by buying kiln time from a local glass studio and starting with only a few tools.

The next section, on basic techniques, clearly and concisely covers how to prepare glass for the kiln, as well as the different things that happen to glass when you heat it. I've included just enough physics to help you understand the processes; once you're familiar with them, you'll be able to plan how to use them in order to get the results you want in your finished work.

The real magic in the book is in the projects. Instead of introducing you to only one or two techniques and repeating those techniques in one project after another, I've made sure that each project presents a new technique that you can use as a jumping-off point for your own imagination and creativity. Just follow the detailed instructions for basic draping, slumping, fusing, making pattern bars, creating flowerpot melts, making fiber-blanket molds—and more. Then take what you've learned, go turn up the heat, and make your own magic. Enjoy!

An Overview

What exactly is kiln forming? Well, a kiln is a very hot oven. When you kiln form glass, you either heat it just enough to make the glass change shape, or you heat pieces of glass so much that they melt and flow together to form a new piece. You can program a kiln to heat and cool in different ways and to maintain spe-cific temperatures for different lengths of time; these segments of a *firing schedule* will allow you to achieve different effects in your kiln-formed work.

Some of the terms used by kiln formers are descriptive and accurate; others can be confusing. Cutting glass, for example, doesn't involve cutting at all. First you *score* the glass (scratch a line in its surface); then you try to bend it along the score line in order to break it. "Slumping" and "draping," on the other hand, indicate exactly what's going on with the glass. You place a piece of glass on top of a concave or convex mold that's been coated with a *release agent* such as *kiln wash* in order to prevent the glass from sticking to it when it's hot. When you fire the glass in your kiln, heat and gravity work to soften the glass just enough to make it slump into or drape over the mold.

Fusing, casting, and *pâte de verre* all require melting the glass. Fusing is the process of placing pieces of glass flat on a kiln shelf that's been coated with a release agent or with a ceramic paper product such as *shelf paper* or *fiber paper.* The pieces of glass are then melted together in very high kiln temperatures. When you kiln cast glass, you melt it in a mold in order to create a solid three-dimensional shape. Pâte de verre (a French term literally translated as "paste of glass") entails making a paste from crushed glass or glass powder and a binding agent, packing the paste into a mold, and melting the glass in the kiln.

In the pages that follow, you'll be introduced to many of the materials, tools, and supplies that kiln formers use and to the basic methods of kiln forming, from preparing your glass for firing to finishing your pieces when they come out of the kiln. Then you'll be guided through the process of making beautiful kiln-formed projects of your own.

Karen Ehart
Dark Teal Male Torso, 2005
29 x 17 x 10 inches (73.7 x 43.2 x 25.4 cm)
Transparent glass; fused, slumped; dichroic
design elements
Photo by artist

Starting Out

This section is divided into four parts. In the first, Materials, you'll find valuable information about glass, as well as metals and mica—two materials that kiln formers sometimes incorporate in their kiln-formed pieces. The second part, Tools (see pages 16–28), offers descriptions of the tools and equipment that are often found in kiln-forming studios. These range from the everyday to the exotic. No need to memorize all this information! Just skim it for the time being and use it as a reference when you select the tools required for the projects you'd like to make. As you develop your skills, you can gradually expand your collection by adding other items.

Supplies (see pages 29–31), the third part, covers both the everyday supplies you'll need, from glass cleaner to paper towels, as well as supplies specific to kiln forming.

Read the last part, Studio Setup and Safety (see pages 32–35), carefully. It will help you design an efficient work area—and work in it safely.

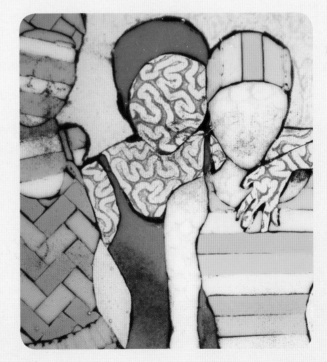

Lesley C.S. Nolan
Bathing Beauties, 2006
18 x 10½ x ½ inches (45.7 x 10.5 x 1.3 cm)
Opal and translucent glass with prefired, assembled, and frit-painted glass; cut, reassembled; fused, polished
Photo by Palette Contemporary Art and Craft Gallery

One of the wonderful aspects of kiln forming is the huge variety of glass with which you'll be able to work, from ordinary window glass to dichroic glass, with its fascinating light-reflecting qualities. Your fired pieces can include more than glass, however. If you make the Sea-Glass Wind Chimes on pages 74–76, for example, you'll incorporate copper rings in the glass so that you can hang the chimes. Or perhaps you'd like to decorate a piece with shimmering mica powders, as demonstrated in the Confetti and Streamers Candy Dish on pages 80–81.

Glass

The primary material used in kiln forming is glass. Long ago, an accidental combination of heat, sand, soda, and lime resulted in the first man-made glass, and for more than 4000 years, people have been making glass objects for ornamentation and trade.

Geri Comstock
Firebird Series, 2001
Diameter, 20 inches (50.8 cm)
Transparent and opal glass; fused, cold worked, slumped
Photo by David A. Comstock

TYPES OF GLASS

Soda-lime glass is the most common man-made glass; its base ingredients are sand, soda, and lime. Traces of iron oxide in the sand cause its typical blue-green color. Other metals and metal oxides can be added to glass to render different colors or change its physical properties. Adding selenium with cadmium sulfide, for example, creates brilliant red. Tin oxide with antimony and arsenic produces an opaque white.

Soda-lime glass is the most popular glass for kiln forming. Many types are available; each has its strengths and limitations. The easiest to use is glass made specifically for kiln forming, which comes in a wide variety of colors and forms, from sheets to fine powders. Several manufacturers produce such glass and provide the technical specifications and firing schedules for it—information that takes a lot of the experimentation and guesswork out of the kiln-forming process and that allows you to make beautiful, durable pieces right from the start.

Lead crystal is glass to which lead oxide has been added in order to make it appear to sparkle more.

Borosilicate glass is often used to make baking dishes. This glass is less affected by changes in temperature than regular soda-lime glass and can withstand both refrigerator and oven temperatures without breaking. Borosilicate is also a favorite glass for *torch workers* (glass artists who manipulate glass directly in a flame) and for some glass blowers.

Float glass (ordinary window glass) is an inexpensive, readily available alternative to commercial kiln-forming glass. This glass is named for the process used to make it. Molten glass is floated on a bed of molten tin to flatten the glass into a perfectly smooth, even sheet. A very thin layer of tin remains on the glass as it cools. Float glass comes in a variety of sheet sizes and thicknesses. Its downsides include the interference, in some kiln-forming processes, of the tin layer on one surface and the lack of variety in colors (the glass is clear). Some glass manufacturers now produce colored glass sheets, paints, and *frit* (crushed glass) that are intended to be combined with float glass.

The dense white of some glassware is the result of the arsenic in it. Boron in kitchenware increases its resistance to temperature changes, and lead makes crystal sparkle. Uranium creates a brilliant yellow color; uranium glass fluoresces under a black light.

Some float glass is *tempered*—a process by which controlled stress is introduced into the glass to make it stronger and also to make it shatter into little pieces rather than into jagged shards if it breaks. (Tempered glass is often labeled with a small, etched logo.) While this glass can be kiln formed, the act of cutting it causes it to shatter. If tempered glass is kiln formed, it loses its tempering and reverts to plain window glass, which can be cut and refired in the same manner as any standard float glass.

If you decide to work only with glass made specifically for kiln forming, you'll have many colors, textures, and even forms of glass from which to choose. Like glass for the stained-glass industry, glass for kiln forming comes in ⅛-inch-thick (3.2 mm) sheets. A wide variety of *opal* (milky in appearance) and transparent solid colors—and even multicolor patterned sheets—is available. Textures range from wavy ripples and bumps to straight lines. This glass also comes in the form of frit in various granularities and as a powder.

Dichroic glass suitable for kiln forming is available in a wide variety of textures, colors, and patterns.

Kiln-forming glass is produced with different surface treatments that affect the way it reflects and *refracts* (bounces and bends) light. *Iridescent glass,* for example, is created by applying stannous chloride or another iridizing solution to molten glass, leaving a thin metal film that is fused to the surface of the glass. The iridescent surface, which can be silver, gold, blue, purple, green, or even emerald or hot pink, reflects light in a way that can change the perceived color of the glass.

Dichroic glass is made by placing glass in a vacuum and vaporizing quartz crystal and metal oxides so that the vapors adhere to the glass surface. This process is repeated many times to yield an extremely thin coating. In spite of the thinness of its surface layer, dichroic glass is brightly colored, and its reflected color is completely different from its transmitted color. The glass may appear to be red if you look at it straight on, but brilliant yellow when you view it from an angle.

Both dichroic and iridescent glass made specifically for kiln forming retain their distinctive colorations during the kiln-forming process. (The iridized surface of some iridescent glass made for the stained-glass industry burns off when the glass is heated.)

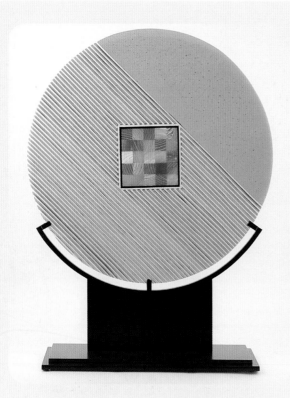

Steve Immerman
Golden Fields, 2006
27 x 19 x 7 inches (68.6 x 48.3 x 17.8 cm)
Kiln-formed glass; strip technique using aperture pour details;
fused and fire polished; gloss surface finish
Photo by artist

GOOD GLASS MATCHES

Not all glasses play well together in a kiln. Unless they're compatible with each other, the resulting piece will break apart either in the kiln during cooling (often spectacularly) or at a later time. Compatible glasses expand and contract at roughly the same rate as they heat and cool. Combining glasses with different shrinkage rates can introduce stress into the finished piece. While stress can make glass stronger, as in the case of tempered glass, in a kiln-formed piece it usually spells disaster.

The term used to describe the rate at which glass expands and contracts is *coefficient of expansion* (or *COE*). To be fused together successfully, two glasses should have the same COE, but there's more to determining compatibility than just COEs, so manufacturers of kiln-forming glass test their glasses to ensure that they're all compatible across colors and opacities. This tested glass is labeled "Tested Compatible." However, most manufacturers only test across their own product lines, so a Tested Compatible 90 COE glass from one manufacturer is not necessarily compatible with a Tested Compatible 90 COE glass from another manufacturer. The most conservative practice is to use only glasses that are Tested Compatible with each other, and occasionally you will still run into problems (see pages 59–60).

Manufacturers produce glass for kiln forming with COEs ranging from 82 (to be compatible with float glass) to 96. Glasses with different COEs shouldn't be combined; use 90 COE glass only with other 90 COE glass. Because float glass isn't tested for compatibility by the manufacturer, it's a good idea to combine float glass only with float glass cut from the same sheet.

But what if you don't know the COE of a glass? Can you kiln form it? The short answer is "yes." All glass is compatible with itself. If you have glass scraps left over from stained-glass projects, for example, as long as they all came from the same original piece of glass, you can cut and fuse the scraps together. You can even crush and then cast this glass in a mold. When you fuse glass of unknown origins, you won't necessarily get the results you expect, but go ahead—experiment and have fun!

Metals

Metals are often incorporated into kiln-formed projects, either for functional purposes or as decorations. To create the Iridescent Pendant (see pages 71–73), for example, you'll learn how to make small silver rings and fuse them between layers of glass so that you can attach a necklace chain to the pendant. When you use metals, you must take into account the type of metal, the amount of metal used in relation to the amount of glass, and the form of the metal, as well.

TYPES OF METALS

Many different metals can be used; each yields different results. The most common are copper, silver, sterling silver, nichrome wire, gold, palladium, platinum, bronze, brass, stainless steel, and iron. Tin, aluminum, and lead are best left to experienced kiln formers, as their melting points are all lower than the melting point of glass, and they either release poisonous fumes or present other problems when they melt. Never use zinc; it also has a lower melting point than glass and releases extremely toxic fumes at kiln-forming temperatures.

Delores Taylor
Hope, 2001
5 x 8 x 8 inches (12.7 x 20.3 x 20.3 cm)
Pâte de verre; kiln cast
Photo by artist

FORMS OF METAL

Wire, foil, leaf, tubing, sheet, rods, mesh, and shavings of different metals can be used for structural purposes or for beautiful effects in kiln-formed projects, but not all metals can be used in all forms. Wire made from most of the metals listed, for example, can be fused into a glass project, but each will react differently to the process. Some will oxidize and change color. Copper and sterling silver turn bluish-green, red, or black when they oxidize. If they're thin enough, gold, silver, platinum, and palladium leaf may vaporize completely, leaving none of the original metal. Some metal will become very brittle. If you're including a metal (other than leaf or foil) for purely decorative purposes, how soft or thin it is doesn't matter. If, however, you want to create wire loops for hanging a fired piece, the metal must be strong enough to bear the weight of that piece.

Mica

Mica is a silicate material often used in kiln forming to give a metallic-looking finish or design component to fused or cast pieces. It can be brushed onto the glass surface dry, mixed into a paste, or applied in a suspension of mica and an agent such as *gum arabic* (see page 29).

Metals surrounding their counterparts in a fused glass piece

Tools

Some kiln-forming tools are commonly found around the home. You'll need to purchase others, but don't rush out to buy everything described here. Each set of project instructions (see pages 64–121) comes with a Tools and Materials list that will let you know what you need.

The Tool Box

Take a look at the lists that follow. The first, Basic Tools and Supplies, includes the items you'll need to make most of the projects in this book. Depending on the project you select, you may also need items from the list below, Add-On Basics; collect these tools as you gain experience. Some kiln-forming tasks are easier and more efficiently executed with the tools named in the third list, Additional and Substitute Tools. While many of the projects in this book can be made without them, a few require their use, and they'll certainly provide you with technical flexibility as you work. Specialized aspects of kiln forming, such as casting, pâte de verre, and applying mica, call for job-specific tools; these are listed in Advanced and Specialty Tools.

Basic Tools and Supplies

Glass cutter
Straightedge
Breaking pliers
Diamond hand pads
Small, motorized grinding tool with assorted glass-grinding bits
Ruler
Pencils
Craft knife
Razor blades
Razor scraper
Awl
Tape measure
Scissors
Bowls in various sizes
Small plastic dishes
Spoons
Dustpan and broom
Black and silver permanent markers, fine-tipped
Circular level
Haik brush
Kiln (or access to one)
Kiln furniture (or access to it)
Molds
Kiln wash and jar
Basic supplies (see page 29)
Basic safety equipment (see page 34)

Add-On Basics

Strip-cutting system
Circle cutter
Wheeled nippers
Running pliers
Tile saw
Glass grinder
⅜-inch (9.6 mm) electric drill
Diamond core drill bits
Standard pliers
Needle-nose pliers
Wire cutters
Hammer
Tweezers
Small hair (or craft) dryer
Airbrush sprayer
Dental picks
Small scales
Funnel
Vacuum cleaner with HEPA filter
Fiber paper in ⅟₁₆-inch (1.6 mm) and ⅛-inch (3.2 mm) thicknesses

Complete glass-cutting system
Basic (or tile) nippers
Grozing pliers
Button-break system
Glass engraver
Round-nose pliers
Jeweler's pliers
Shelf paper
Fiber blanket
Fibrous silica shelf cloth

Ring saw
Band saw
Drill press
Handheld glass grinder/polisher
Lap grinder
Wet-belt sander
Sandblasting system
Mesh screens
Pillowcases
Canvas bag
Frit crusher
Paintbrushes
Make-up spatulas
Flowerpots

Cutting and Breaking Tools

In order to work with pieces of glass, you'll cut out the shapes you want by scoring the glass with a glass cutter and breaking the glass along the score lines.

Glass cutters are available in a dizzying number of variations, from wheel and grip designs to self-oiling capabilities and neon colors. Color aside, some of these variations make a real difference in how well you cut glass and, consequently, in how much you enjoy the process.

The best way to choose a cutter is try out a few at a stained-glass supply shop. You might like a pistol-grip cutter, or you might prefer a traditional, handheld upright cutter. I use both types, but all my cutters have self-oiling, tungsten carbide cutting wheels.

A strip-cutting system is a must if you enjoy the precision of working with strips of glass. Some of these systems come with specialized cutters or cutting wheels as parts of their setups. Others provide only a guide mechanism for uniform measuring and cutting. A straightedge used in conjunction with a handheld cutter will do the same job, but not with the same efficiency.

Circle cutters, some of which also cut ovals, come in several styles and sizes. Some have small, steel-wheeled turrets, and others have the same high-end tungsten carbide wheels that the more expensive handheld cutters have. Two features to look for in a good circle cutter are smoothness of motion and stability. I prefer a circle cutter that allows me to make the entire score in a single motion; not having to let go of the tool prevents the cutter's pivot point from shifting or tipping while I'm scoring.

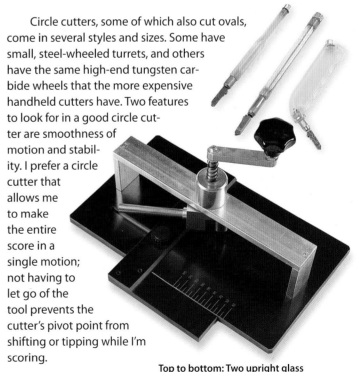

Top to bottom: Two upright glass cutters, a pistol-grip glass cutter, and a small circle cutter

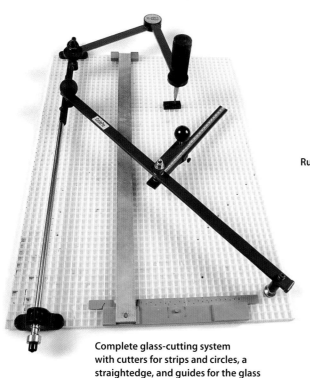

Complete glass-cutting system with cutters for strips and circles, a straightedge, and guides for the glass

Grozing pliers

Running pliers

Breaking pliers

Wheeled nippers

Basic (or tile) nippers and a button-break system

A complete glass-cutting system includes a cutting surface, an attached straightedge, and attachments for cutting precise angles, strips, and circles. It's invaluable for production cutting of geometric pieces.

Sometimes you can break scored glass by using only your hands; at other times, additional tools are necessary.

Breaking pliers, which have two flat, smooth jaws, are common in many studios. The best types produce a break that is exactly perpendicular to the surface of the glass.

Wheeled nippers bite pieces of glass from a sheet and are used for mosaic and other chunk work. You hold them like scissors and line up the wheels at the edge of the glass, in the direction you want the break to go. Then squeeze them together with firm pressure, and the glass will snap cleanly apart. The wheels may rotate freely or may be fixed.

Basic (or tile) nippers are also used to bite off pieces of glass from a larger piece. Unlike wheeled nippers, however, the cutting ends of these nippers are perpendicular to the handles.

Grozing pliers are similar to breaking pliers, but one or both of the jaws is curved, and both are serrated. The

versions with one flat jaw can double as breaking pliers; make sure the flat jaw is facing up when you use them in this way. The curved jaw is used to scrape off small, uneven bits of glass from the edges of the break.

Running pliers, which come in a variety of styles and materials, work as a fulcrum to break the glass by applying equal pressure on both sides of a score. They're used on any glass (especially thick glass) that requires a little more pressure than usual to break. Inexpensive plastic versions will only *run* straight scores (see page 38 for a description of running a score). Higher-end aluminum or steel models can be manipulated to run a score along an inside curve.

A button-break system, either handheld or mounted on a cutting surface, works much like running pliers. You position the scored glass over a convex button and run it by applying even pressure to the glass on both sides of the score with either a handheld device or your hands.

More sophisticated glass-cutting tools are also available. An inexpensive tile saw from a hardware or home-improvement store, is an excellent one; it's good

Ring saw, with diamond-coated wire blade

for cutting both glass and *mullite dams* from broken *kiln shelves* (mullite is a durable, low-COE, aluminosilicate mineral; see pages 26–27 for descriptions of dams and shelves). A water-cooled tile saw helps keep down the dust and will cut thick pieces of glass with ease. Because it has a round, flat blade, this tool can only make straight cuts.

A ring saw, which is water-cooled and chips less than a standard tile saw, can cut any imaginable shape out of glass. The blade is a thick, diamond-covered wire ring that cuts in any direction; all you have to do is press the glass against the blade. While a ring saw is the tool of choice for making curved cuts in thin glass, it isn't suitable for cutting very thick pieces, such as the pattern bars in the Pattern-Bar Mirror Frame (see pages 112–15).

A band saw can cut a wide range of shapes, including gentle curves, and can also cut thick pieces of glass, but it can't handle the more intricate patterns that a ring saw can.

When you make a cut with any kind of saw, you lose the width of the blade (or *kerf*) from your cut material. A tile saw has a larger kerf than a ring or band saw, so it wastes more glass. Chipping from the blade can also be more pronounced than with a ring or band saw.

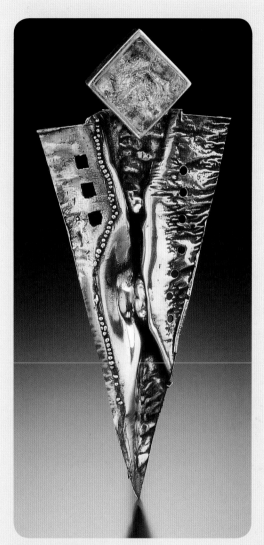

Nancy Goodenough
Voices of the Earth, 2005
3 x 1¾ x ⅜ inches (7.6 x 4.4 x 1 cm)
Bullseye glass (soda lime), dichroic Firestone glass; kiln formed, cold worked, fire polished, fold formed, granulated sterling silver
Photo by Hap Sakwa

Small, motorized grinding tool in a drill press

Glass grinder

Grinding, Polishing, and Drilling Tools

Tools for grinding, polishing, and drilling holes in glass projects range from simple abrasive pads to stationary electrical equipment.

When you grind or polish glass, you must keep wet the area of the glass that contacts the grinder or polishing tool. Water minimizes the release of ground silica into the air (be sure to read the information in Studio Setup and Safety, starting on page 32) and also lubricates the grinding surface, which helps it to last longer. Many of these tools come equipped with water reservoirs or piping for an incoming water source. Those that don't should be used under running water or with a bowl of water on hand for frequent wetting and rinsing.

Diamond hand pads are the most important tools in the kiln-forming toolbox. These rubber, sponge-sized pads are the least expensive and most versatile of all the grinding and finishing tools. The diamond grit on their surfaces comes in different degrees of coarseness, ranging from a very coarse 60 grit to a very fine 3500 grit. Because the pads are soft and flexible, they conform to rounded edges better than the flat, hard bits and wheels used with electric tools.

The stationary glass grinder, frequently used in stained-glass work, is also handy for preparing glass for kiln forming and for

Diamond hand pads

cleaning up the edges of fired work. It's relatively small and includes a water reservoir with a sponge that cools the grinding bit. The bits come in grits from 60 to 325. Standard bits are usually 100 grit, coarse bits are around 60 grit, and fine bits are 220 to 260 grit.

A ⅜-inch (9.6 mm) electric drill will help you with finishing work (see pages 57–58). You may want to purchase a drill press as well; it will hold your drill bit steady so it won't slip on a glass surface.

Diamond core drill bits to fit electric drills are available from specialty suppliers and are used to drill holes in glass. These bits are hollow tubes, the inner and outer surfaces of which are coated with diamonds at the bottom. When you drill a hole in glass with a diamond core bit, the bit removes a circle of glass that's the same diameter as the bit's interior and leaves a hole in your glass piece that's the same diameter as the bit's exterior.

Diamond core drill bit chucked in electric drill

A small, motorized grinding tool, available from many hardware and home-improvement stores, and an assortment of diamond, other abrasive, and felt bits will help you grind and polish areas that are inaccessible to larger tools; they can also be used to drill holes. The diamond tips are available in grits from 120 to 325. The polishing points are finer (325 to 600 grit), and the felt pads are for use with *cerium oxide* (a polishing compound). A water-soaked sponge will help cool and lubricate the tip during use.

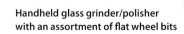

Handheld glass grinder/polisher with an assortment of flat wheel bits

Steve Immerman
Eleuthra, 2006
8 x 12 x 22 inches (20.3 x 30.5 x 55.9 cm)
Kiln-formed glass; strip technique using aperture-pour details;
fused, wheel textured and slumped; polished edge;
satin surface finish; in matte, black (metal stand)
Photo by artist

A handheld glass grinder/polisher is good for grinding and polishing the surfaces of pieces that are too heavy or unwieldy to pick up. Most of these grinders have a water-feed system that hooks up to a hose or another water source, so you must use them outdoors or in a special "wet" area of your studio. This tool comes with both a diamond wheel and a wooden one, and attachable resin and felt polishing pads. The diamond wheel is used to remove large amounts of glass from the surface, and the wooden wheel, which has a hook-and-loop surface, is used with polishing pads to smooth and polish glass.

A lap grinder is most useful for its ability to simultaneously grind and polish long edges or large, flat surfaces. It can be used with pieces of glass that extend over its edges but works best when the entire glass edge or flat surface is in contact with the tool's grinding surface. Wheel diameters range from 6 to 22 inches (12.2 to 55.9 cm). Water-fed models are available in horizontal and vertical orientations. Magnetic-backed pads, in grits from 40 on up to felt pads for polishing, adhere to the steel lap wheel. Avoid recycling water in your lap grinder; debris in it can scratch your piece and wear out the wheel quickly. Catch the water runoff in a bucket, let the debris settle, and then pour only the water down the drain. Throw the sludge into the trash.

A wet-belt sander has belts instead of wheels and is used to smooth and polish the edges of glass. These sanders come in tabletop and floor models, and in horizontal and vertical orientations. Like lap grinders, they're made with either reservoir systems or direct hookups for water.

Ask two kiln formers which is better—a lap grinder or a wet-belt sander—and you're likely to get two completely different answers. Choosing high-end finishing tools is often a matter of personal preference and exposure. Both tools offer advantages; the best way to decide between them is to try them out at a retail glass show or local supply shop.

Although diamond hand pads can remove *devitrification* from the surfaces of your projects and stubborn kiln wash that sticks to their bottoms, a sandblasting system makes those jobs easier. (Devitrification is the unwanted formation of crystals on the surface of glass.) Sandblasting is also a great way to selectively remove the iridized surface from glass prior to firing it and to create a smooth, matte finish on fired glass. While etching products do work on kiln-formed glass, sandblasting provides a deeper, more even coverage. Etching and carving your fired pieces with a sandblasting system are two finishing techniques that can add a creative dimension to your work.

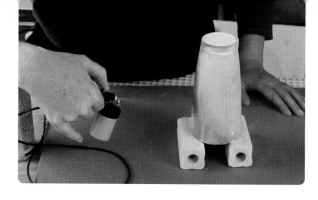

Miscellaneous Tools

Though you won't need them all for every project, the following tools are staples in the glass-studio toolbox: a ruler, pencil, craft knife, standard pliers, needle-nose pliers, wire cutters, hammer, razor blades, razor scraper, awl, tweezers, tape measure, and scissors. Also found in many households—but not usually in toolboxes—are bowls in various sizes, small plastic dishes, spoons, a small hair (or craft) dryer, toothbrushes, and a dustpan and broom.

Use fine-tipped black and silver permanent markers for marking on glass. They're resistant to washing and grinding, and you won't have to remove all the ink by hand later; many kinds will burn off during firing. Test all markers to find out which ones burn off in the kiln and which ones don't. The ink in the white markers used by some glass manufacturers doesn't burn off and can leave an unexpected, permanent mark when your project comes out of the kiln.

A circular level will help you make sure a kiln shelf or mold is level in all directions. You don't want to open the kiln after firing and find that your piece is unevenly shaped because your shelf or mold wasn't level.

An airbrush sprayer (see photo above) is invaluable for applying kiln wash to metal and finely detailed molds. It's also useful for achieving a thin, even coat of *overspray* (a substance used to prevent devitrification) on glass.

An inexpensive glass engraver is handy for signing and dating your work, even if you don't plan to kiln form professionally.

A haik brush, readily available from all kiln-forming suppliers, consists of a handle made from several pieces of bamboo, with clumps of long, soft, fine hairs coming out of each one. This brush provides superior coverage when you're applying a release agent to a kiln shelf, as it

Haik brush

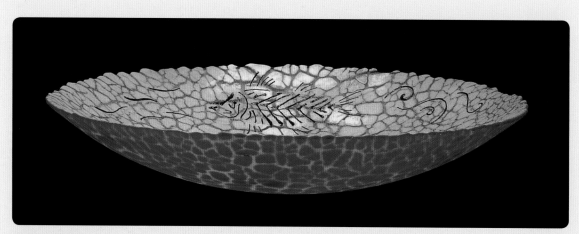

Bob Leatherbarrow
Fish Bowl, 2005
15 x 3 inches (38.1 x 7.6 cm)
Bullseye opal powder; fused and slumped, sandblasted
Photo by artist

leaves a smooth surface that's virtually free of brush marks.

Dental picks work well for cleaning kiln wash out of nooks and crannies in your fired glass and are often available free for the asking from your dentist.

Dental picks

Round-nose pliers and smooth-jawed jeweler's pliers are useful for working with soft metal wire.

Small scales allow you to calculate the volume (by weight) of glass that you'll need in order to create a final piece of the desired size. Pieces of cut glass change size when they're fired; measuring the length and width of every one can be tedious, and frit can't be measured this way at all. Food scales work well for glass weighing up to 2 pounds (907 g); postal scales provide approximate weights for large amounts of glass.

Round-nose pliers

A funnel is useful for pouring substances such as frit, powders, and chemicals back into their storage jars.

To stay on top of the mess generated by kiln form-ing, you can use a dustpan and broom, but a small vacuum cleaner with a HEPA filter will keep much of the harmful dust out of your lungs by sealing it away. Don't use a regular vacuum cleaner; it will shoot the smallest glass particles right back into the air—and maybe into your lungs.

Specialty Tools

Specialized kiln-forming techniques require special tools. If you make your own frit, for example, you'll need different sizes of mesh screen in order to separate the frit into different sizes. You'll also want to have plenty of old pillowcases and a canvas bag on hand to contain the glass when you make frit by smashing the glass into chunks or crushing it. Although commercial frit crushers are available, the pillowcase-and-hammer method that I use to beat glass into tiny pieces on the cement floor of my studio is an inexpensive alternative (see page 93). It's also good exercise and a great way to relieve stress!

A variety of paintbrushes is useful for working with frits and glass powders. Make-up spatulas are excellent tools for techniques that require precise placement of crushed or powdered glass.

Cynthia Oliver
A la Carte, 2002
22 x 17 x 1½ inches (55.9 x 43.2 x 3.8 cm)
Opaline glass; fused, sand-blasted; organic, 24-karat gold-leaf inclusions; Bullseye and Uroboros glasses, fused, slumped
Photo by Keith Proctor

Kilns

The most important tool you'll use in kiln forming is the kiln itself, so you want to make sure that you get the right one for your purpose. The first distinction to make is between kilns made for ceramics and kilns made for glass. While you can kiln form glass in a ceramic kiln, using a kiln designed for glass will give you better results.

Ceramic kilns are primarily *side firing* (the heating elements are in the sides of the kiln), and they're more likely to be tall and narrow than long and shallow. Unless you're casting or making jewelry, most of your work will require firing flat pieces of glass. To keep the glass from breaking as it heats or introducing stress into it as it cools, its entire surface should be heated and cooled at the same rate. In a side-firing kiln, the middle of the glass rests farther away from the elements than its edges do, which can result in *thermal shock* from uneven initial heat-up. (Thermal shock is breakage caused by rapid or uneven heating or cooling.)

Exposing all the glass to the kiln's heating elements at about the same distance helps it to heat evenly. For

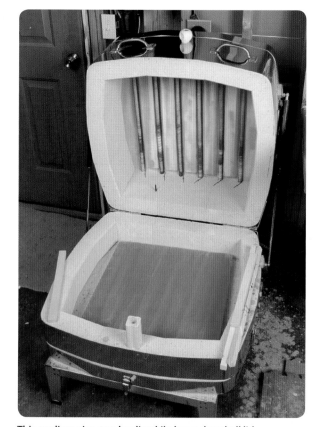

This medium-size, top-loading kiln has a clamshell lid.

this reason, most glass kilns are *top firing* (the elements are in the top), or top and side firing rather than just side firing, and are relatively shallow. You can develop firing schedules to use with ceramic kilns, but it's easier to use a glass kiln instead.

Glass kilns are available in a wide range of sizes. Their insulation can be *firebrick* (a lightweight refractory ceramic material), ceramic fiber blanket, ceramic board, or a combination of these materials. Most commercially available glass kilns are electric, but there are some gas models.

Different kilns are loaded in different ways. Some have flat lids that open upward, others have doors on the front, and still others have clamshell or bell lids. Your choice will be based largely on personal preference, but front-loading kilns are the easiest to use by yourself when you're manipulating the glass during firing.

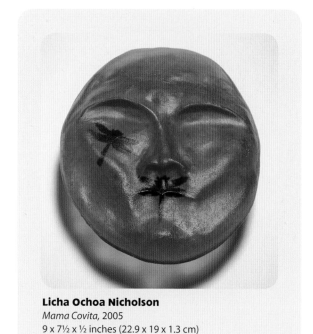

Licha Ochoa Nicholson
Mama Covita, 2005
9 x 7½ x ½ inches (22.9 x 19 x 1.3 cm)
Cast glass with copper inclusions
Photo by Lynn Nicholson

Modern kilns come with computerized controllers that make it easy to set up a firing schedule from start to finish.

KILN TEMPERATURE-CONTROL FEATURES

Most new kilns now come with *computerized controllers* that allow you to program all the different stages of a firing in advance. For each stage, you can set the number of degrees that you want the kiln to advance each hour (or minute), the desired temperature, and the amount of time you want the kiln to stay at that temperature.

Ellen Abbott and Marc Leva
Marsh Mallow Honey, 2005
5½ x 5½ x 5½ inches (13 x 13 x 13 cm)
Transparent glass frit; pâte de verre, kiln cast
Photo by Thomas Riley Gallery

SELECTING A KILN

How should you choose a kiln? At first, you might not even need to buy one. Many local pottery and glass kiln-forming studios rent kiln space and tools. Another good way to get your feet wet is to take a class and check out the teacher's kiln. When you're ready to purchase your own, select one large enough to handle the projects you want to make ("large enough" means deep enough, too), but not so large that you don't want to fire it because it's not full.

Kiln Furniture

Although other materials are also used, most traditional *kiln furniture*—the various items used inside the kiln—is made from mullite. Mullite is extremely durable and strong, and its very low COE helps it resist thermal shock when it's exposed to rapid heating or cooling.

Firebrick, which is used as an insulating material in many kilns, is easily carved and cut, and can be used to make kiln furniture and molds. This material can stick to fusing or slumping glass, however, so shouldn't be permitted to come into contact with it.

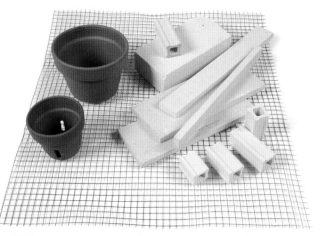

Kiln furniture includes posts for propping up kiln shelves and glass, dams to contain molten glass, and terra-cotta flowerpots to fill with glass scrap or frit and heat until the glass flows out the hole in the bottom.

KILN SHELVES

Kiln shelves provide adjustable-height firing surfaces for the glass in the kiln. They're commonly available in three different materials, each of which has advantages and disadvantages.

Mullite shelves hold and transmit heat more than shelves made of other materials. They're the most read-

Laurel Yourkowski
Sailing, 2002
35 x 34 inches (88.9 x 86.4 cm)
Dichroic glass; fused
Photo by artist

ily available (they're used in both ceramic and glass applications), are reasonably inexpensive, and produce an even, flat surface on the bottom of the glass. Mullite shelves are also very strong; they're designed to be moved around fully loaded and won't break, even when bearing significant weights. They resist scratching and warping, and are the heaviest by volume of the three types of shelves. The largest size available commercially is approximately 1 x 24 x 24 inches (2.5 x 61 x 61 cm). To prevent glass from sticking to mullite shelves during firing, you must use a release agent with them.

Ceramic fiberboard shelves have become popular in recent years. This insulating material for high-temperature applications (it's used as the insulation in some kiln lids) isn't subject to thermal shock, conducts very little heat, and is extremely lightweight. Ceramic fiberboard shelves are available in larger sizes than mullite or *vermiculite* shelves—up to 1 x 36 x 48 inches (2.5 x 91.4 x 122 cm).

Ceramic fiberboard comes in different degrees of toughness, but all of it scratches, dents, and breaks easily. A fiberboard shelf placed on *kiln posts* (used to support shelves in the kiln) can break from the weight of the pieces fired on it.

From top: Kiln shelves made of mullite, ceramic fiberboard, and vermiculite

However, the shelves can be treated with a rigidizer to make them harder and less subject to surface nicks and dents. They produce the roughest surface on the bottom of the glass, and they can warp. Some kiln workers claim that glass will stick to ceramic fiberboard at fuse temperatures, but I routinely fire on two different kinds of fiberboard shelves that have not been rigidized, without using a release agent, and have experienced no problems with sticking.

The weight and heat-retention properties of vermiculite shelves rest somewhere between those of mullite and ceramic fiberboard shelves. Vermiculite shelves produce a very smooth, even surface on the bottom of the glass. They're more fragile than mullite shelves and crumble around the edges, but they don't dent as easily as most ceramic fiberboard shelves. They do absorb moisture, which can gas off during a fusing cycle and show up as large bubbles in the middle of a fused piece. They also stick to glass, so you must place fiber paper or shelf paper between the shelf and glass, or use a powdered release agent when fusing on them. Two-inch-thick (5.1 cm) shelves can be supported on kiln posts and are less likely to warp than the 1-inch-thick (2.5 cm) sizes.

KILN POSTS AND DAMS

Kiln posts are not only useful for holding up kiln shelves and molds; they also make good wedging supports around dams. Dams are placed around glass to keep the glass a specific size when you're casting or creating thick work. Although you can buy dams made from mullite and other materials, you can also make your own from broken kiln shelves. Many pottery supply stores sell broken shelves at discounted prices; just cut these up with an inexpensive tile saw or one rented from your local home-improvement center.

FLOWERPOTS

A terra-cotta flowerpot can be used as a crucible to hold glass as it melts; the glass then flows out of the hole in the bottom of the pot. The Orchid Melt Sculpture on pages 101–4 is an excellent example of how to use a flowerpot in this way.

Carol Carson
Together, 2006
26 x 26 x 6 inches (66 x 66 x 15.2 cm)
Bullseye glass; kiln formed
Photo by artist

Molds

To shape glass by using a mold, you can slump it into a concave mold, drape it over a convex mold, or cast it inside a mold to create a three-dimensional piece. Molds are made from many different materials.

CERAMIC MOLDS

The most common slump molds are made from ceramic and are relatively inexpensive. Fashioning your own by hand or on a potter's wheel is easy but outside the scope of this book. However, good books on the subject are available. Porcelain, terra cotta, or other clay bodies may all be used. The only disadvantages to ceramic molds are their weight and fragility. They can be very heavy, they're subject to thermal shock when they're cooled too quickly, and they chip and break easily.

Clay slip (a liquid form of deflocculated clay) also makes good slump, drape, and casting molds, as it is lightweight, smooth in texture, and durable.

Avery H. Anderson
Hummingbird Platter (Animal Medicine Series), 2003
20 x 20 x 2½ inches (50.8 x 50.8 x 6.4 cm)
Dichroic and opaque glass; fused, sandblasted, slumped; micas and gold lusters
Photo by artist

Unlike solid casting molds, slip molds are hollow, so they don't hold heat the way solid molds do. Objects cast in slip molds therefore cool evenly from all sides, which allows you to use a faster, simpler firing schedule than any you'd use if you had to take into account the difference in cooling rates between exposed and insulated surfaces.

You should prepare ceramic molds with kiln wash (see page 54) before using them, or they can stick to glass during firing. You can reuse molds for many slump firings before you need to prepare them again, but you should reprep casting molds after each firing. Slump molds that could trap air between the mold and the glass during firing should also have holes in their bottoms to allow air to escape during firing.

METAL MOLDS

Stainless steel molds work best, but people who make glass sinks and very large bowls sometimes use inexpensive carbon steel woks as slump molds. A wok will usually work three or four times before heating and cooling torque it out of shape.

Metal molds must be coated with a release agent. See page 54 for tips on how to apply kiln wash to metal molds. Another release agent that's used on metal molds is *boron nitride* (see page 30).

FIBER-BLANKET MOLDS

Fiber blanket (see page 31) makes good slump and drape molds when it's treated with a special hardener. Creating a fiber-blanket mold is covered in the Lace Wall Sconce project on pages 108–11.

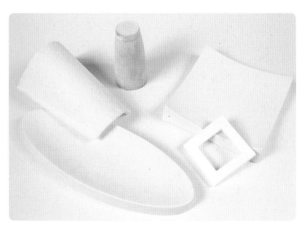

Clockwise from top: Molds made from metal, ceramic slip, ceramic fiberboard, ceramic slip, and hardened fiber blanket

Supplies

Supplies for kiln forming range from the exotic, available only from specialty retailers, to the mundane. Some are essential, and others are required only occasionally.

Everyday Supplies

You'll want to keep the basic supplies listed below on hand at all times. Each set of project instructions in this book will specify the additional supplies that you need. If you're missing any of the items in this basics list, just make a trip to your local grocery and home-improvement stores.

Basic Supplies

Glass cleaner	Sponges
Dishwashing detergent	Green nylon scrub pads
Glass adhesive	Fine steel wool
Adhesive remover	Fine-grit sandpaper
Cotton swabs	Masking tape
Paper towels	Toothbrushes
Dishcloths	Toothpicks
Towels	Plastic scrub brush

Specialty Supplies

Like any other craft, kiln forming requires some special supplies. Described in this section are the ones that are most commonly found in kiln-forming studios.

Oversprays, which come in lead-bearing and non-lead-bearing forms, help prevent or repair devitrification on the surfaces of your fused pieces. Lead-bearing oversprays aren't food-safe and should never be used on pieces intended to hold food. You can brush an overspray onto glass, but you'll get more even coverage, without brush marks, if you spray it on with an airbrush sprayer.

Cerium oxide is a polishing compound used with cork or felt polishing pads and the tips on motorized polishers. It comes in both rust-colored and white

MATERIAL SAFETY DATA SHEETS

If you want detailed information about the contents of your chemicals and refractory materials, material safety data sheets (MSDS) are excellent sources. They list the ingredients and the hazards associated with the contents, they recommend safe handling and disposal procedures, and they can help you make informed decisions about whether or not you want to use those materials. You can get MSDS information from your materials supplier or from manufacturers; many are also available online.

powders and is mixed with water to make a slurry for polishing.

Several kinds of glass-etching compounds are available, in both paste and dip form. These chemicals will etch patterns into glass; some are better suited than others to glass made for kiln forming.

Fuser's glue is mixed with frit or glass powder to make a paste for pâte de verre (see the Pâte de Verre Sugar Square project on pages 82–83) and can also be used to hold cut pieces of glass in place until they're fused together. This glue burns off during firing and leaves no residue on the glass.

Gum arabic is used to hold mica powders and glass enamels in suspension. It burns off cleanly during firing, it isn't as thick as fuser's glue, and it isn't colored. (Gum arabic is used in the Confetti and Streamers Candy Dish project on pages 80–81.)

Almost everything done to glass in a kiln requires the use of a release agent to stop the glass from sticking to the surfaces of kiln shelves or molds. Kiln wash—the most readily available and least expensive of the release agents—adheres well to ceramic shelves and molds. Kiln wash made for use with glass comes as a powder

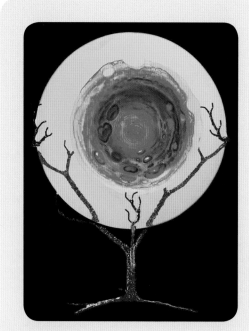

Rick Jarvis
Amber Singularity, 2006
24 x 20 x 8 inches (61 x 50.8 x 20.3 cm)
Spectrum glass; kinetic cast
Photo by Richard Nicols

Shelf paper is a heat-resistant ceramic material that is placed on kiln shelves in order to prevent glass from sticking to them. It comes in 41-inch-wide (1 m) rolls or 20 x 20-inch (50.8 x 50.8 cm) sheets that don't need to be prefired or treated in any way prior to use. The organic binders that hold the paper together burn off during firing. Although shelf paper is marketed as a single-use product, you can reuse it as long as it provides intact coverage of the kiln shelf.

Shelf paper shrinks a little during firing and may not be suitable for larger kiln-formed pieces. It also reacts adversely to some types of iridescent glass. In addition, the paper can create a milky white film on the underside of opal glasses if the binders aren't vented during burn-off, so I usually vent the kiln to 1000°F (538°C) when I use it with opals. (For more information on firing, see pages 42–47.)

Fiber paper, which is made from alumina-silica fibers and an organic binder, is used in the same manner as shelf paper. It comes in ¹⁄₁₆-, ¹⁄₈-, and ¼-inch (1.6, 3.2, and 6.4 mm) thicknesses. The thickness you use depends of what you want to do. In the Iridescent

and is either mixed in a ratio of one part kiln wash to five parts water (measured by volume) or sprinkled dry on the kiln shelf. When used wet, it's applied with a haik brush or an airbrush sprayer to the shelf or mold.

Several types of kiln wash are available from different manufacturers. Some must be scraped off the kiln shelf after firing; others can be wiped off with a damp sponge. Kiln wash usually includes a coloring agent that burns off during firing so you can tell if a shelf has been fired or not by its color.

Boron nitride is another separating (or release) agent and is often applied to metal molds and shelves. It comes in powdered, liquid, and aerosol forms.

Aluminum hydrate is a powdered release agent that is sprinkled on kiln shelves; it can be brushed off after firing.

Among the firing-related products that kiln formers use are kiln wash in powdered form and (from top to bottom) fiber blanket, shelf paper, fiber paper in two different thicknesses, and fibrous silica shelf cloth.

Pendant project (see pages 71–73), for example, ⅟₁₆-inch (1.6 mm) paper is used to support the silver loops at the height of the ⅟₁₆-inch-thick (1.6 mm) glass. In the Split-Leaf Philodendron Fountain project (see pages 116–121), ⅛-inch-thick (3.2 mm) fiber paper is used to create the bas relief on the fountain bowl and plates.

The binder in fiber paper, like the binder in shelf paper, makes it stiff. After the binder burns off during firing, the paper softens, but it doesn't fall apart completely as shelf paper does. Handle this paper carefully; you can use it as long as it holds up. In order to burn off the binders, some people vent their kilns to 1000°F (538°C) the first time they fire fiber paper, but I've never seen a benefit to doing this. One note of caution: At temperatures over 1800°F (982°C), the alumina-silica fibers in this paper can convert to cristobalite, a known carcinogen.

Fibrous silica shelf cloth is an alternative to kiln wash and shelf papers that provides a beautiful, woven-cloth texture to the underside of your finished work. Each side of the cloth has a different weave. The cloth is usually good for 10 or more firings before you have to discard it. Don't use this material for firings above 1500°F (816°C), as the glass can melt deeply into its fibers at higher temperatures, and the cloth will tear when you remove the glass. Like fiber paper and fiber blanket, fibrous silica shelf cloth is partly converted to cristobalite when subjected to temperatures in excess of 1800°F (982°C). Always cool shelf cloth to room temperature before removing the glass, so as not to weaken or tear the cloth.

Fiber blanket is similar in composition to fiber paper but is thick, soft, and fluffy rather than flat and stiff. It comes in ½-inch (1.3 cm) and 1-inch (2.5 cm) thicknesses and is an excellent insulator; it's the insulating material in some glass kilns. Fiber blanket can be used to help kiln-formed projects cool uniformly after annealing, and if it's treated with a hardener, can also be used to make slump and drape molds.

Carol Carson
Girlgold, 2006
26 x 6 x 6 inches (66 x 15.2 x 15.2 cm)
Kiln-formed Bullseye glass; welded steel base
Photo by artist

Use glass-shipping crates to store your glass, and cover their tops to provide an extra work surface.

Lights, Water, Action!

Your glass-preparation area for kiln forming should be comfortable, easy to clean, and have plenty of full-spectrum light and a place to wash your glass. You may get so caught up in working with glass that you're not conscious of the hours passing by—but your body will certainly notice if your work area isn't ergonomic.

I like to stand while I work; my tables are all about waist height, so I don't have to stoop or reach more than

necessary. My floor is concrete, which is very easy to clean but hard on the feet and joints, so I've covered it with thick rubber mats. These are no trouble to sweep, and they provide good support and cushioning. Avoid carpet in your work area; small bits of glass and dust from kiln wash and shelf paper will mess it up really quickly.

Even though my studio is windowless, it's so brightly lit that on cloudy days it looks sunnier inside than it does outdoors. I like fluorescent light because it's bright, inexpensive, and cool; my kilns generate enough heat as it is. However, regular fluorescent bulbs don't emit enough red and green light to reflect the full light spectrum. This flaw is most evident when you look at a glass color such as neo-lavender. Under regular fluorescent light, the color appears to be light blue, but the same color viewed outdoors in sunlight or under an incandescent light is a beautiful lavender. Fortunately, fluorescent lights come in full-spectrum and "daylight" varieties that serve as excellent studio lights.

Another important component of the kiln-forming studio is running water—or at least a wash-out area where splashed water won't harm anything. The best way to clean your glass before firing it is with a little dishwashing detergent and a lot of water. These remove fingerprints, oils, dust, and almost every other contaminant that might otherwise ruin your piece in the kiln. Some people like to wash large pieces in a shower stall or the bathtub, and smaller pieces in a sink or laundry tub. I have a big, three-bin, stainless-steel restaurant sink with an overhead hanging sprayer; it's one of the best purchases I've ever made.

There's no doubt about it: kiln forming glass is messy. Bits of glass and ground glass end up on the tables and floor, and dust from the kiln wash, shelf paper, and fiber paper end up everywhere. You need not only surfaces that are easy to sweep and wipe clean, but also a storage system that will keep your glass, tools, and supplies as dust-free as possible. I love clear plastic boxes with snap-on lids. They're inexpensive, stackable, and sturdy, and they come in a wide variety of sizes. The grocery-store versions designed for food storage, available in ½- to 13-cup (118 ml to 3.1 L) sizes, are indispensable for frit, jewelry findings, and other odds

Plastic boxes with snap-on lids, stacked on wire shelves, make wonderful storage containers for scrap glass, frit, jewelry findings, and many other odds and ends.

Rick Jarvis
Olive Chaos Theory, 2006
24 x 20 x 8 inches (61 x 50.8 x 20.3 cm)
Spectrum glass; kinetic cast
Photo by Richard Nicols

and ends. Storage and organization stores often carry a shoebox size and a 15-quart (14.2 L) size that are great for glass scrap. I carry my work around in the 30-quart (28.4 L) size.

I recommend organizing all your plastic boxes on commercial-grade wire shelves. They're sturdy enough to support a lot of weight, easy to assemble, and adjustable, and they don't catch as much dust as solid shelves.

Full sheets of glass should be stored upright. The crates in which retailers ship these sheets make excellent storage containers; they're just the right size and shape to protect the glass from breakage. And if you're tall, the tops of the crates make great work surfaces.

Don't Run with Scissors

Staying safe and sound when you work with glass is a combination of common sense and education. You already know that running with scissors is dangerous and that protecting your lungs from airborne particulate matter is a good idea. On page 34 is a list of critical safety items that you should keep in your work area—and use. I keep the safety equipment that I use most often—gloves, plastic safety glasses, particulate respirators, a chemical respirator, and earplugs—strategically stashed around the studio so that no matter where I am, I always have what I need close at hand. Descriptions of these and other safety-related items, as well as useful safety tips, follow.

Basic Safety Equipment

Plastic safety glasses
Particulate respirator
Chemical respirator
Chemical-resistant gloves
Rubber dishwashing gloves
Heat-resistant gloves rated to 2000°F (1093°C)
Adhesive strip bandages

GLOVES AND GLASSES

Purchase a pair of asbestos-free, silica-based, wool-lined gloves to protect your hands from temperatures up to 2000°F (1093°C). Even though you can kiln form glass without ever touching anything warmer than room temperature, you may occasionally need to open a kiln as hot as 1700°F (927°C). Oven mitts won't protect your

hands from temperatures this high; indeed, the mitts would probably burst into flames.

These gloves are thick and somewhat cumbersome to wear, so you should also have a good pair of general-purpose, heat-resistant gloves that are rated to handle materials up to 500°F (260°C). You'll use them when you open and close the kiln lid, remove and replace peep-holes, and perform similar tasks.

To protect your hands from caustic chemicals, such as those used to etch glass and remove stubborn adhesives from it, buy a pair of chemical-resistant gloves from a home-improvement or hardware store. Be sure to follow the recommendations for protective covering that are printed on the labels of any chemicals you use.

The fiber-blanket insulation in many glass kilns contains silica; touching it can cause skin irritation and rashes on some people. I'm one of those people, so I keep rubber dishwashing gloves next to the kiln and wear them (and my particulate respirator) whenever I clean the kiln after a firing.

If you find that you're often looking into the hot kiln, invest in a pair of retinal safety glasses that will protect your eyes from both harmful UV (ultraviolet) and IR (infrared) rays. Typical didymium safety glasses are great

Safety equipment is a must in the studio. Shown here are two different kinds of high-temperature silica fiber gloves, another rated to 500°F (260°C), noise-canceling headphones, rubber gloves, a particulate respirator, a chemical respirator, adhesive strip bandages, and earplugs.

Whenever you clean your kiln, be sure to wear a particulate respirator. If the kiln insulation is fiber blanket, you may also want to wear rubber gloves and a long-sleeved shirt to protect your skin from irritation.

for UV protection, but they won't shield your eyes from IR rays when you peer into a hot kiln.

Wear plastic safety glasses whenever you cut or grind glass; chips will fly. I like the wraparound ones, as they protect my eyes from the sides as well as from the front.

RESPIRATORS

Depending on the work you do, two kinds of lung-protection devices will be necessary: a particulate respirator and a chemical respirator. Both are available at home-improvement and hardware stores. Always wear the particulate respirator when you work with frit or are cleaning ceramic fiber products after firing them. Whenever there's a risk of ground glass being airborne, it's time for a particulate respirator. The chemical respirator is just for use with chemical fumes.

CLOTHING, HAIR, AND JEWELRY

Synthetic fibers can react badly when they're exposed to high temperatures. The last thing you want is to fuse your shirt to your skin when you open the kiln to do a little high-temperature manipulation. A long-sleeved cotton shirt will protect your arms from heat exposure for a few minutes of open-kiln time. For longer exposures, consider wearing a denim jacket (remove any metal buttons) or reflective, heat-resistant sleeves made specifically for this purpose. Remember, too, that moving tools and equipment can catch long hair (keep it tied back) and grab hanging jewelry (take it off).

EAR PROTECTION

Grinders, etchers, compressors for sandblasting, and many other noisy tools can damage your hearing over time. Traditional foam earplugs and noise-canceling headphones are both inexpensive ways to protect yourself in most situations. Check the frequency rating of your power tools; if any are higher than 120 dB, you should wear earmuffs designed to protect you from very loud noises.

William Zweifel
Spill, 2003
8 x 8 x 12 inches (20.3 x 20.3 x 30.5 cm)
Hand-woven glass
Photo by Larry Sanders

BANDAGES

This may seem obvious, but glass is sharp! Every time you cut glass, you create a fresh, sharp edge. Pay attention, don't get complacent, and be careful not to touch those edges. And face it: if you work with glass long enough, you're going to cut yourself, so keep a box of adhesive strip bandages in your work area. Clean any cuts thoroughly, slap on a bandage when necessary, and keep going.

Kiln forming is an art that's based on relationships—yours with the glass you select and with your kiln, and your kiln's with the glass you fire in it. Once you're comfortable with these relationships, you'll be well on your way to producing beautiful kiln-formed work.

This section will guide you through every basic aspect of those relationships, from cutting the glass for your projects all the way to finishing your fired work and troubleshooting common problems. By the time you've finished reading these pages, you'll understand what happens to the glass that you fire in a kiln, why it happens, and how you can control what happens by using different kiln-firing methods and firing schedules. You'll also know how to prepare your glass, kiln shelves, and molds for successful firings, and how to finish your fired glass pieces.

As in most good relationships, information and practice go a long way toward achieving satisfaction. This section provides the information; the projects that follow it will provide you with plenty of opportunities to practice.

Barbara Muth
Beneath the Blanket Fort, 2005
14 x 14 x 1 inches (35.6 x 35.6 x 2.5 cm)
Kiln-formed glass
Photo by Bart Kasten

Cutting Glass

To score glass, first you use a glass cutter to scratch a thin line on its surface. Then you try to bend the glass along the score line. Instead of bending, the glass will snap apart. The score serves as both a starting point for the break and as a guide for the break to follow.

Holding the Cutter

A pistol-grip glass cutter is held like a pistol or garden sprayer. An upright cutter can be held with your thumb and index finger, and stabilized against your middle finger as if it were a pen, or held between your index and middle fingers, and gripped with your thumb, index, and middle fingers. Any cutter, no matter how you hold it, will only score properly if you keep the wheel perpendicular to the glass surface.

Scoring the Glass

You can stand or sit while you score glass, but you should be comfortable and able to see the spot where the cutter wheel touches the glass. A clear view is especially important when you're cutting around a pattern adhered to the glass; you must be able to score right up to the pattern's edge.

The cutting wheel should be clean of all debris and lubricated with cutting oil. Make sure the glass is clean, too, and placed on a clean, flat cutting surface, with the smoothest side of the glass facing up. Glass chips or other debris beneath the glass can cause it to break when you press down on it during scoring.

Some people like to pull their cutters toward themselves, and others prefer to push them away. Certain glass cutters are designed to be used one way or the other. I find that pushing a pistol grip cutter is easier than pulling it. If you pull, your hand can obscure your view of the wheel.

To score the glass, hold the cutter firmly but not too tightly. Starting at one edge of the glass, roll the cutter across to another edge, pushing the tool downward gently and evenly. (The score should run from one edge to another to provide a continuous guide for the break.) As you roll the cutter, you'll know you're exerting just the right amount of pressure if you hear a gentle

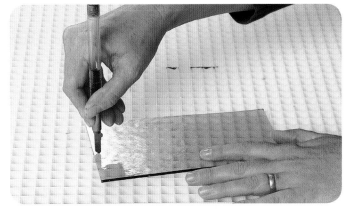

There are two common ways to grip an upright cutter;…

…no matter which hand position you choose, keep the cutter perpendicular to the glass as you make the score.

Pushing a pistol-grip cutter away from you rather than pulling it toward you enables you to keep an eye on the cutting wheel.

scratching sound. If you don't hear anything, you're not pushing down hard enough. If you hear what sounds like a fingernail being scraped across a blackboard, you're exerting too much pressure.

Just before the cutter reaches the other edge of the glass, decrease the pressure slightly; lift the cutter lightly off the glass as it reaches the edge. Letting the cutter wheel drop off onto the cutting surface will dull it.

Running the Score and Making the Break

Breaking the glass is a process that happens in stages. First, the glass begins to run (separate) between the score on the top surface and the bottom surface of the glass, and from one end of the score to the other. Then the glass separates into two pieces. Sometimes the run and the break happen so quickly that you can't distinguish between them. At other times, you can slowly and carefully run the score and then break the glass apart. (Running the score before breaking it helps control the direction of the break.)

There are several ways to run and break a score. You can use your hands to run and break at the same time. You can run the score while the glass is flat on the cutting surface, then pick up the glass to break it. You can use breaking pliers, or you can use running pliers or a button-break tool. The method you choose will depend on several factors: how thick the glass is, how far the score is from the edges, and whether the score is a relatively straight line or a tight curve.

Breaking by Hand

With ⅛-inch-thick (3.2 mm) pieces of glass that are small enough to hold comfortably with both hands, if the score and the edge of the glass don't form a very sharp angle, if the score isn't a tight curve, and if the areas of glass on both sides of the score are large enough to grip comfortably, you can break the score by using only your hands. Position your hands and the glass as shown in the top photo on the opposite page, with the scored side of the glass facing up. Push gently upward with your index fingers while you push down with your thumbs, as if you were trying to bend the glass upward along the score. As you apply even pressure, you should hear a little pop. If your pressure is light enough, this pop will indicate that the score is starting to run. Now press harder to complete the break.

For more complex scores (wavy lines and long, gradual curves, for example) that are too far from an adjacent edge of the glass to reach with breaking pliers, you may want to run the score before breaking it. This method works best if the glass is transparent and light enough in color to see through.

Place the glass with the score face down on the cutting surface. With the heel of your palm, push gently down directly above the score, anywhere along its length. As you do this, you should hear a pop and see the run come up through the glass, just beneath the spot you pressed. To continue the run, move your hand along the score to another spot and push down gently again. Repeat until the entire score has run. Then carefully pick up the glass, turn it over so the score is face up, and break the score with your hands.

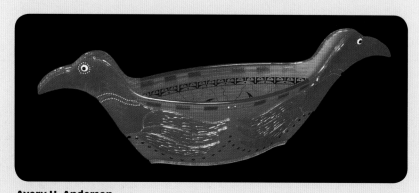
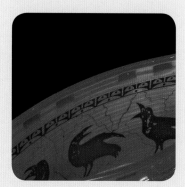

Avery H. Anderson
Raven Spirit Vessel, 2006
10 x 28 x 5½ inches (25.4 x 71.1 x 14 cm)
Opaque glass; fused, slumped, sandblasted; enameled imagery
Photo by artist

Breaking with Tools

If the score is within ½ inch (1.3 cm) of the edge of the glass, the easiest way to snap it is to use a single pair of breaking pliers. The following instructions are for right-handed people. If you're left handed, just switch the right and left designations.

Hold the glass in your left hand, with the score facing up and oriented toward you; the score should be at the edge of the glass on your right-hand side. Hold the breaking pliers in your right hand. Position the ends of the jaws parallel to and right up against one end of the score; the handles of the pliers should be perpendicular to the score. (If you're using combination breaking/grozing pliers, make sure the flat jaw is on top of the glass, and the curved jaw is underneath.)

Press straight down on the back of the pliers, while lifting up their front end. Your goal is to apply upward pressure on the bottom of the glass, under the score. You should hear the pop as the score starts to run; the glass may break at the same time, or you may need to apply more pressure. On longer pieces, only a portion of the score may begin to run. If that happens, move your pliers down along the score, either to the place where the score hasn't run yet or as far as your pliers can reach and still rest right up against the score. Use the pliers to apply pressure to this new spot. If necessary, repeat in another spot until the glass has separated completely along the score line.

When a glass piece is too small or too long and narrow to hold in your hands, you can use two pairs of breaking pliers. Align the two pliers so that the ends of their jaws face each other across the score; then apply pressure to both pairs of pliers simultaneously. This technique is also useful for separating two or more scored strips that have broken off together as a single piece.

If the glass is quite thick, the score is complex, or the score is too far from the edge to use breaking pliers, use a button-break system or running pliers. Running pliers apply even pressure to the top and bottom surfaces of the glass. How you use either tool will depend on the type you've purchased. Follow the manufacturer's instructions for best results.

To break a score by hand, first place your index fingers underneath the glass, on either side of the score line, and position your thumbs as shown here.

To break the glass along the score, push gently upward with your fingers as you push down with your thumbs.

Running pliers apply equal pressure along both sides of a score in order to break out the glass.

Scoring and Breaking Tight Curves

A good, straight score line provides a path of least resistance along which glass can break easily. With a tightly curved score, however, the glass will break along the score until it reaches the tightest portion of the curve and then tend to ignore the rest of the score, breaking straight across unscored glass to an edge instead. This tendency makes it difficult to cut tight curves in glass—but not impossible.

To cut these curves successfully, you must first divide the glass that's inside the inner curve of the main score into smaller sections by scoring a series of half-moon-shaped pieces, each no wider than ¼ inch (6.4 mm). Then you break out each smaller section individually. The length of each section is also important; it's easier to score and break short, gradual curves than it is to break long, sharp ones. Dividing a tight curve into several smaller pieces will allow you to cut curves that would otherwise be impossible without using a ring saw.

Tight inside curves are easier to break out if you make multiple scores inside the curve and break these smaller pieces out first.

Cutting Glass to Fit Patterns

When you want to cut glass to match a pattern, either attach the pattern to the glass with double-sided tape or spray adhesive and score around it, or trace around the pattern with a black or silver permanent marker and score along the marked line. If the glass is transparent

Barbara Muth
Early Morning Contemplation, 2004
15 x 5 x 1 inches (38.1 x 12.7 x 2.5 cm)
Kiln-formed glass
Photo by Bart Kasten

and light enough in color, you can set the glass on top of the pattern and trace the pattern outline onto the glass surface. Whenever possible, position the pattern so that the most difficult cut is closest to the edge of the glass, leaving room to move the pattern back a bit and try again if your first cut breaks poorly. Make the most difficult breaks first and always remember to score from one edge of the glass to another.

Cutting Strips, Ovals, and Circles

Strips, ovals, and circles can be cut with a freehand glass cutter, but it's easier to use cutters designed specifically for these shapes. As with running pliers, how you use these cutters depends on what kind they are; just follow the manufacturer's instructions.

Because the score for a circle or an oval is continuous and doesn't go from one edge of the glass to another, you'll need to make additional scores, out to the edges of the glass, in order to break out the circle. Making the circle score at least 1 inch (2.5 cm) from the nearest edges of the glass minimizes the risk of leftover glass on the circle's edges.

Even with opaque glasses, I find that the easiest way to cut a circle is to score the glass on one side, flip it over, and run the scores with the heel of my hand until the pieces around the circle break off. Start by scoring the circle on a square of glass. Then make four scores, each perpendicular to the circumference of the circle

and running out to the edge of the glass, at the three, six, nine, and twelve o'clock positions. This is the one instance in which I don't score from edge to edge. Instead, I begin the score on the outside of the circle, a little way from the circle score, and then I score to the edge of the glass. The small gap between the scores helps prevent the glass from breaking across the circle and ruining it. Turn the glass over. (If the glass is opaque, remember where the circle score is positioned.) Now run the circle score by pressing down with the heel of your hand at the two, four, eight, and ten o'clock positions. When the circle score has run all the way around, press down in the middle of each score that runs out from the circle. If your scores were good and you pressed hard enough, the four pieces around the circle should pop off without your having to pick up the glass and break them.

Now that you're familiar with the tools and supplies you'll use in kiln forming and with the art of cutting glass, I'll introduce you to firing schedules—and then we'll dive right into how you can create beautiful, unique pieces of glass art.

Diane Anderson
Fire, 2005
26 x 20 x ¼ inches (66 cm x 50.8 cm x 6.4 mm)
Opaline frit glass, kiln formed, hand finished
Photo by Larry Sanders

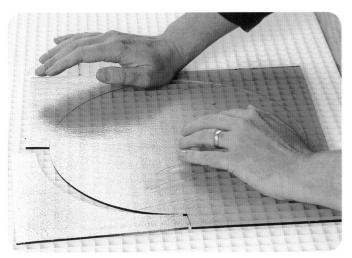

After you've scored a circle, turn the glass over and run the score by pressing down on the score lines with the heel of your palm.

Firing Schedules

Intrinsic to every kiln firing is a schedule that tells you at what rate to increase or decrease the kiln temperature from one point to the next (the *ramp*), what the ending temperature should be at each point (the *level*), and how long the glass must be kept at that temperature (the *hold*). Although a firing schedule can be written out as text, it's easier to present and read as a table, with the ramps named R1, R2, R3, and so on; and the levels and holds designated as L1, L2, and L3, and H1, H2, and H3, respectively. Take a look at the Sample Firing Schedule on the opposite page.

The ramp rates in this schedule are shown in degrees per hour, but some kiln controllers express them in degrees per minute. To convert the rates in this book to minutes, just divide the degrees by 60.

There's usually one point in every firing schedule at which the rate is "as fast as possible"; it's indicated by "AFAP" in the firing schedule. Different kiln controllers program AFAP in different ways. Some use "0," and some use "9999." I use both types of controllers, so I just write AFAP in my schedules and logs. Another difference between controllers is how they handle hold times that are longer than one hour. One of my controllers will accept up to three hours, expressed in minutes (180 minutes), but I have to enter any greater length of time as both hours and minutes. Another kiln accepts only minutes. My best advice here is to read the manual that comes with your kiln.

The firing schedules in this book are labeled as "basic" because there is no single firing schedule that will always work for a particular task. Firing schedules depend on many factors, including the kiln you use, the glass you use, the placement of the kiln shelf, how many times the piece has already been fired—and more. These basic schedules are a good place to start and are resources that will help you develop your own schedules.

Delores Taylor
Venus, 2001
6½ x 14 x 14 inches (16.5 x 35.6 x 35.6 cm)
Pâte de verre; kiln cast
Photo by Jerry McCulloum

From the start of your kiln-forming journey, you should keep a written record of every firing. Write down your firing schedule and in the Notes column, record what kind of shelf or mold and release you used, where the shelf—and mold, if you used one—was placed (on the floor or on posts), and if it was on posts, at what height. Also record anything else that might help you or someone else troubleshoot a problem. When a fired piece turns out spectacularly, you'll want to know what you did so that you can replicate it. If you open the kiln during the firing, in the appropriate row of the Notes column, mark both the kiln's temperature when you opened it and how long you kept it open. At the end of the firing, if problems such as bubbles, devitrification, or hazing occurred (see pages 60–62), record that information in the last column.

Another good reason to log your firings is that different kilns process at different temperatures. I use three different kilns on a daily basis, and each one has a slightly different full-fuse temperature (see Fusing on pages 48–51). When I want to use one kiln to reproduce a piece created in another, I use my log to put together an appropriate schedule.

The Stages of a Firing

Although you don't need to understand the physics of firing in order to create kiln-formed projects, the more you understand about firing, the fewer problems you'll have to face as you develop your skills. Treat this section as a reference; it will prove helpful as your work progresses.

As glass is heated in a kiln, it goes through a series of physical changes. The graph on the next page, Stages in a Fuse Firing for 90 COE Glass, offers an example of the stages of one type of firing. These changes don't happen at distinct, measurable temperatures. Instead, the glass softens, melts, flows, and hardens again within

SAMPLE FIRING SCHEDULE

STAGE	FAHRENHEIT / CELSIUS	NOTES
R1	300°F (167°C)/hour	The rate at which the kiln temperature is increased or decreased from room temperature; shown here in degrees per hour
L1	1250°F (677°C)	The target temperature for the first ramp (R1)
H1	45 minutes	The length of time to hold at L1 target temperature before moving to the next ramp
R2	600°F (333°C)/hour	The rate of increase or decrease in temperature from L1 to L2
L2	1500°F (816°C)	The target temperature for R2
H2	10 minutes	The length of time to hold at this temperature before moving on to the next ramp
R3	AFAP	The abbreviation for "As Fast As Possible"
L3	960°F (516°C)	Notice that the R3 in this case moves toward a lower target temperature.
H3	60 minutes	The final hold
R4	Off	Cool naturally to room temperature.

STAGES IN A FUSE FIRING FOR 90 COE GLASS

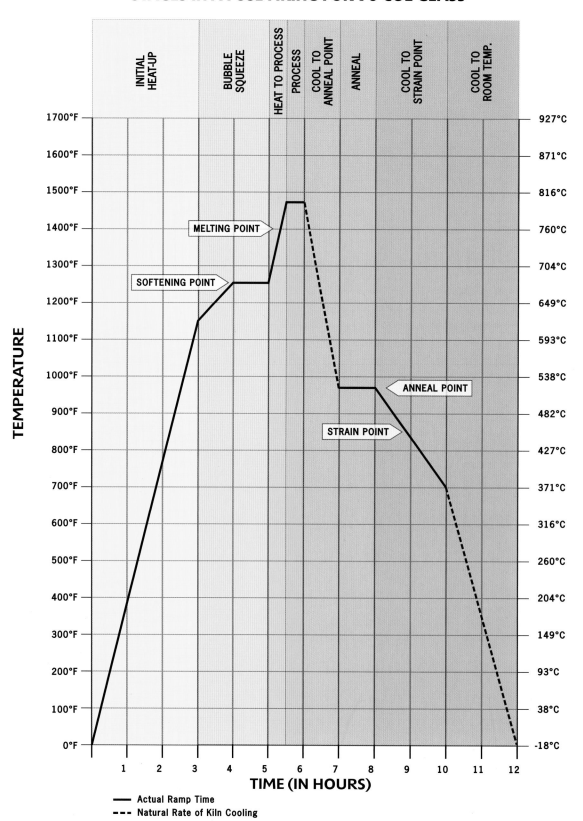

temperature ranges. For the sake of convenience, we assign a specific temperature to a change in the glass; we know that this change happens at approximately that point and not exactly at it. The four temperatures that we care most about are the *softening, melting, anneal,* and *strain* points.

Each of these points is roughly associated with a change from one stage of a firing to another. As the graph shows, each firing has six basic stages: *initial heat-up, process, cool to anneal point, anneal, cool to strain point,* and *cool to room temperature.* I usually add two more stages to fuse firings: *bubble squeeze* and *heat to process*; they occur between the initial heat-up and process stages.

INITIAL HEAT-UP

The first stage of a firing is the initial heat-up. If you move too quickly through this stage, you risk thermal shocking the glass and cracking or breaking it. You may need to vent the kiln during this stage, as it's the one during which organic materials such as the binders in fiber paper, shelf paper, and glues burn off.

Richard La Londe
Blue Moon, 1986
14 x 19 x 21 inches (35.6 x 48.3 x 53.3 cm)
Fused Bullseye glass slumped into a stainless steel mold
Photo by artist

HOW TIMES DO CHANGE

Thanks to the ubiquitous computerized controllers found on most modern glass kilns, you now have a lot of control over how you fire glass. When I started kiln forming (right after I finished walking to school barefoot in the snow, uphill both ways), I had to set an infinite control switch (a manual switch that must be reset at each stage of the firing) on medium or high and watch the little needle on the pyrometer that told me how hot the inside of the kiln was. When it was hot enough, I turned the kiln off and opened it up until it cooled down to the annealing range. Then I closed the lid and set the controller to low and my kitchen timer to one hour. When the timer went off, I turned off the kiln. The process was simple—and so was the level of complexity of my fired pieces, but my firing logs were very complicated.

Instead of recording what I was going to program into the computerized controller, I had to log what I actually did: how many times I turned the heat up or down manually, at what stage the firing was when I did that, and how long everything was taking. I figured out my ramps after the fact by dividing the degrees of temperature change by the number of hours each ramp took—and as you might guess, the rate wasn't constant in those ramps. I have great respect for the artists who were turning out complex pieces in those days. If you're working with an infinite switch, you'll need to keep meticulous records in order to learn your kiln well enough to make it follow complex firing schedules.

BUBBLE SQUEEZE

In slump and drape firings, the initial heat-up stage ends at the softening point, when the glass begins to sag and fall. Then the process stage begins. In fuse firings, the softening point is in the middle of the bubble-squeeze stage. Moving slowly through the bubble-squeeze stage and holding the temperature at the end of it allows time for the glass to succumb to gravity slowly, squeezing out most of the bubbles from between layers of glass and from between the glass and the kiln shelf.

HEAT TO PROCESS

Between the bubble-squeeze stage and the process stage in a fuse firing, there are still a couple of hundred degrees Fahrenheit (about 93° Celsius) to move through. While you can't thermal shock a piece in this temperature range, you can end up with some enormous bubbles in the middle of your piece if you're firing on very smooth kiln shelves and you move too quickly through it. Unless I have a compelling reason to do otherwise, I take my time and fire at 400°F (204°C) per hour.

PROCESS

The process stage is the temperature range during which the real action of the firing takes place. In a slump firing, it's the stage during which the glass sags into

Martin Kremer
In Depth, 2006
17 x 17 x 3 inches (43.2 x 43.2 x 7.6 cm)
Fused, kiln formed, cold worked
Photo by Tommy Olaf Elder

the mold and assumes its shape. In a fuse firing, it's the stage just after the melting point, when the glass softens enough to melt and flow together. For melts and other high-temperature firings, the process stage begins at temperatures a bit above the melting point, when the glass flows freely—more freely than it does in a normal full fuse.

COOL TO ANNEAL POINT

After the process stage, the glass cools down to the anneal point. There's no reason to move slowly through this stage. You can't introduce stress into the glass by rapid cooling at this stage if you anneal properly at the end of it. However, moving too slowly through it can create problems, as this is when devitrification (see pages 52 and 61–62) usually happens. A good rule here is to cool as quickly as possible. Some people crash-cool their kilns by opening them up until they cool to the anneal point; I usually let mine cool as quickly as it will naturally with the lid closed.

ANNEAL

Once the glass has reached the anneal point, it should be held there long enough to stabilize the temperature throughout the entire piece; this is the anneal stage. The thicker the glass, the longer it will take for the temperatures to equalize throughout it. You can't over-anneal a piece, so err on the side of taking too long rather than not long enough during this stage. It doesn't matter which process came before the anneal stage (how high the temperature was); the thickness of the glass is what determines the duration of the anneal stage.

All the basic firing schedules in this book include annealing schedules for pieces ¼-inch (6.4 mm) thick—the standard thickness of soda-lime glass when it's left to flow unimpeded and the approximate thickness of two standard-thickness pieces of kiln-forming glass. When I fire something thicker (measured at the thickest area of a piece); I typically add 30 minutes to the annealing time for every additional ⅛ inch (3.2 mm)—or single thickness of glass.

In theory, the surface dimensions (diameter, or length by width) of a piece don't matter in the annealing schedule, but in practice the way a kiln heats may not be perfect. Cold spots and drafts in kilns can make achieving an even temperature throughout difficult. I find that covering castings and very thick, dammed pieces, such as the pattern bars in the Pattern-Bar Mirror Frame (see pages 112–15) with 1-inch-thick (2.5 cm) fiber blanket as the glass moves into the anneal stage helps to even out the temperature of the piece as it cools.

COOL TO STRAIN POINT

Again, changes in glass don't occur at specific temperatures. The anneal stage is the stage during which you hold a constant temperature in the kiln in order to reach equilibrium in the glass temperature, but the process of annealing continues all the way down to the strain point of the glass. At the strain point, the atoms stop moving around, and no more stress can be introduced into or removed from the glass. Because the glass is still annealing as it cools to the strain point, when the glass is ¼-inch (6.4 mm) thick or thicker, I program a set cooling rate so that I can control how fast the kiln cools during this stage, instead of letting it cool naturally. I am also very conservative in my cooling schedules and go well below the actual strain point in the cool-to-strain-point schedule to ensure that the glass has cooled evenly.

COOL TO ROOM TEMPERATURE

Below the strain point, during the cool-to-room-temperature stage, I usually let the kiln cool naturally. If I've fired a very thick, dammed piece or casting, I've already covered it with fiber blanket in order to insulate it (see the preceding Anneal section) so it will cool slowly enough. Letting thick pieces cool completely to room temperature is very important. To avoid having the glass break from thermal shock, I try to allow a very thick piece to sit for a day outside the kiln, at room temperature, before I do anything more to it.

Lisa Allen
Boxed In, 2005
20 x 21 x 4 inches (50.8 x 53.3 x 10.2 cm)
Soda-lime glass; fused and slumped; pattern bar
Photo by artist

Now that the scientific stuff has been covered, you can move on to the art. There are many ways to create glass art in a kiln. The basic firing techniques introduced in this section are slumping, draping, fusing, and fire polishing. In some of the projects (see pages 63–121), casting, melting glass onto a shelf, and pâte de verre are also covered.

Slumping

To slump glass, you place it on top of a concave mold and heat the glass just enough to make it slump into and shape itself to the mold. (A good example of a slumped project is the Faux-Weave Lattice Plate shown on page 66.) As long as you anneal the glass properly at the end of the firing, virtually any single piece of glass can be slumped; because you're only working with one piece of glass, compatibility isn't an issue.

The Basic Slump Schedule that I use for ¼-inch-thick (6.4 mm) COE 90 and 96 glasses is shown on this page. You can tweak the top hold temperature and time based on your kiln's performance. The top surface of slumped glass is unaffected by the mold's surface, but the bottom of the glass often picks up some of the detail from the mold's interior. One way to minimize this effect is to hold very low slump temperatures for a very long time.

Draping

Draping glass is similar to slumping in terms of the temperatures required and the action of the glass, but instead of falling into a concave mold, the glass drapes around a convex mold. So why would you choose to drape glass instead of slump it? When you drape glass, any mold marks are left on the inside of the piece rather than on its exterior. If you're making a lampshade, for example, you might want to drape the glass so the finished outer surface will be shiny and scuff free. Another reason to drape is to achieve the look of draped fabric (see the Floral Draped Vase and Votive on page 64). For draping, use the Basic Slump Schedule.

Fusing

The third and most varied kiln-forming technique is fusing. Fusing encompasses everything from lightly sticking two pieces of glass together to melting different glasses together completely in order to form a single new piece. Three general categories of fusing exist: *tack fusing*, *partial fusing*, and *full fusing*. Figures 1, 2, and 3 on the next page show two pieces of glass fused together to each of these extents.

When glass is placed on a concave mold and fired, it slumps into the mold's interior.

BASIC SLUMP SCHEDULE

STAGE	FAHRENHEIT / CELSIUS
R1	400°F (222°C)/hour
L1	1265°F (685°C)
H1	20 minutes
R2	AFAP
L2	960°F (516°C)
H2	60 minutes
R3	150°F (83°C)/hour
L3	700°F (371°C)
H3	Off

Figure 1

Figure 2

Figure 3

Although a lot is going on in the glass at the atomic level during kiln forming, you don't need a degree in physics to kiln form glass. All you really need to know is that as glass heats and moves into a liquid state, its atoms begin to move around freely. Atoms like their space; once an atom is able to move around, it will keep moving until it achieves an optimal distance between itself and each of its neighbors. The placement of atoms on the surface of glass is actually determined by the atoms in the interior. This effect is called *surface tension* and is one of the factors that determines how thick glass will be as a liquid. *Viscosity* (a liquid's resistance to flow) and *specific gravity* (or density) are two other factors that contribute to determining the thickness of the glass.

If you heat a ⅛-inch-thick (3.2 mm) piece of soda-lime glass long enough and to a temperature high enough, it will form a wafer about ¼ inch (6.4 mm) thick. This "ideal" thickness for soda-lime glass has caused many people to claim that you can't place two pieces of glass side by side in a kiln and fuse them into a single ⅛-inch-thick (3.2 mm) piece. But physics can be our friend. You can fuse a single thickness of glass if you under-stand what's happening as it heats and flows—and plan accordingly.

Consider this example: If a ⅛-inch-thick (3.2 mm) piece of glass wants to be ¼ inch thick (6.4 mm) in liquid form, as it heats, it will *bead up* (or pull inward). Two pieces of ⅛-inch-thick (3.2 mm) glass placed side by side in the kiln will tend to pull up and away from each other before they have a chance to fuse together. The trick to fusing these pieces into a single ⅛-inch-thick (3.2 mm) piece is to overlap them slightly as you lay them out—or to be happy with the open, lacy, partial adhesion you'll get when you position them side by side. The creation of a really complex ⅛-inch-thick (3.2 mm) piece may require multiple firings.

One final thing to consider when you fire glass ¼ inch (6.4 mm) or less in thickness is that the edges of a piece this thin will pull in and up, giving the finished piece a rolled-edge look, much like the raw edges on sheets of stained glass. Unless you like that look, single-thickness fusing is best done with a top fuse temperature a little lower than that required for a full fuse.

Ellen Abbott and Marc Leva
Egg Cup 1, 2004
4¼ x 4 x 4¼ inches (10.8 x 10.2 x 10.8 cm)
Transparent and opal glass frit; pâte de verre; kiln cast
Photo by artist

When you want to fuse two or more pieces of glass into a single thickness, overlap them slightly so their edges won't bead up and pull away from each other during firing.

TACK FUSING

When you're planning the look of a finished piece, it helps to know how the glass will flow as it fuses. In a tack fuse, the thickness of the final piece will be about the same as the combined thicknesses of all the pieces before firing. The goal in a tack fuse is to heat the glass just enough to make the surface tacky. At this stage, contiguous pieces of glass stick together without changing their basic shapes (figure 1 on page 49). The Basic Tack-Fuse Schedule provided on this page is the schedule for tack fusing two single-thickness layers of glass, one on top of the other. Note that the thickness of the piece at its thickest spot determines the required anneal time. (For more details, review the Anneal section on pages 46-47.)

PARTIAL AND FULL FUSING

As you take glass to higher temperatures and hold it there for longer periods of time, it will melt and flow together more and more (figures 2 and 3 on page 49). The glass will look like a puddle of melting ice cream right up to the last point at full fuse. If you start with pieces of different sizes, layered in stacks of different heights, before full fuse you'll see little lumpy bits protruding above the surface where the top layers were. Full fuse occurs when the surface is uniformly flat.

Unfortunately, I also find that full flat fuse is the point at which a host of annoying problems can happen, so I tend to stop my firings just short of that point. Generally, for pieces in which the surface was more or less level before the firing, there isn't much difference between the way my fired piece looks and the way it would have looked had I taken it all the way to a full flat fuse. But when I stack several small pieces on a larger base so that different areas of the starting piece are radically different in thickness, the thicker starting portions usually end up a little thicker at the end of the fuse.

Why do I stop short of a full flat fuse? Because the glass really flows at that point, and the extra volume of the layered pieces has to flow somewhere. The glass stack melts down to the thickness of the base, and the extra glass from the stack sloshes out and deforms the edges. When you stop just a bit short of full flat fuse, little mounds of glass will remain in the stacked areas, but most of the molten glass that has been dispersed into the base just makes the whole piece a bit thicker; it doesn't have a chance to flow out and deform the edges as much.

In addition, when glass flows completely, any air bubbles that were trapped in it are free to move around; they move up and out if they can. The result can be a

BASIC TACK-FUSE SCHEDULE

STAGE	FAHRENHEIT / CELSIUS
R1	400°F (222°C)/hour
L1	1300°F (704°C)
H1	5 minutes
R2	AFAP
L2	960°F (516°C)
H2	60 minutes
R3	150°F (83°C)/hour
L3	700°F (371°C)
H3	Off

BASIC FUSE SCHEDULE

STAGE	FAHRENHEIT / CELSIUS
R1	400°F (222°C)/hour
L1	1150°F (621°C)
H1	0 minutes
R2	150°F (83°C)/hour
L2	1250°F (677°C)
H2	60 minutes
R3	400°F (222°C)/hour
L3	1465°F (796°C)
H3	20 minutes
R4	AFAP
L4	960°F (516°C)
H4	60 minutes
R5	150°F (83°C)/hour
L5	700°F (371°C)
H5	Off

finished surface with many little popped-bubble craters on it. Unlike the spaces left by air bubbles that pop up through water, which are filled in so quickly you can't even see where they were, popped bubbles in glass usually don't heal. Instead, they leave little craters behind. And I don't like craters.

The Basic Fuse Schedule is the one I use with my 22-inch-square (55.9 cm) interior, top-firing, clamshell kiln, and my 14-inch (35.6 cm) octagonal, top- and side-firing kiln. The schedule I use with my 36 x 72-inch (91.4 x 182.9 cm) coffin kiln has a top fuse temperature that is 25°F (4°C) lower.

The differences in full-fuse temperatures among my kilns make it worth repeating here that every kiln fires a little differently. You'll need to play around with your own kiln and the schedules provided in this book to match the desired outcome of a firing. These schedules provide a basic jumping-off point for you. They're not set in stone—not even for me. Even a change in kiln shelf height offers an adventure in fine-tuning.

Fire Polishing

Fire polishing is the process of heating a glass piece that has a roughened surface (from grinding or sandblasting, for example) just enough to soften the surface and make it shiny again. (The checkerboard shown on page 98 has been fire polished.) This change won't happen at temperatures as low as you use to slump, but you don't need to go up to full-fuse temperatures, either. Use the Basic Fire-Polish Schedule.

Before you can kiln form glass, you'll need to take some steps to ensure successful results.

The edges of both these glass squares were ground to remove imperfections. The square at the left was then fire polished to make the edge shiny again.

BASIC FIRE-POLISH SCHEDULE

STAGE	FAHRENHEIT / CELSIUS
R1	400°F (222°C)/hour
L1	1350°F (732°C)
H1	10 minutes
R2	AFAP
L2	960°F (516°C)
H2	60 minutes
R3	150°F (83°C)/hour
L3	700°F (371°C)
H3	Off

Richard La Londe
Mystic Messenger, 1994
42 x 28 inches (106.7 x 71.1 cm)
Fused Bullseye glass with dichroic and gold leaf
Photo by artist

Preparing Glass

Glass is an *amorphous solid*; in other words, it doesn't have a crystalline structure. The silica in glass is fickle, however, and given the opportunity, will devitrify, becoming less glasslike and forming crystals. These crystals aren't pretty; they show up as a scummy, hazy, rough area on the surface of your fused piece. Dirt is one of the main causes of devitrification. Give the crystals something around which to form (dirt is ideal), and they will. To help prevent devitrification—and oily fingerprints fused like decorations onto the surface of your piece—wash and dry all your glass before fusing it.

Another way to help prevent—and even fix—devitrification is to apply an overspray to the surface of the glass. Although you can brush it on, I like to apply mine with an airbrush sprayer. Some oversprays can be used at lower slumping temperatures, but others (including the lead-free, food-safe ones) must be processed at fusing temperature. One of the most popular oversprays is simply powdered glass in an alcohol suspension; the alcohol evaporates, and the thin layer of glass powder or enamel creates a new surface on the glass.

Preparing Kiln Shelves

Most kiln-shelf materials will stick to melted glass, so you need to either treat the shelf with kiln wash before firing or use a ceramic paper product between the glass and the shelf. (Ceramic fiberboard is the shelf-material exception to this rule for me.) The most common kiln shelves are made from mullite; more release products are available for these shelves than for ones made from

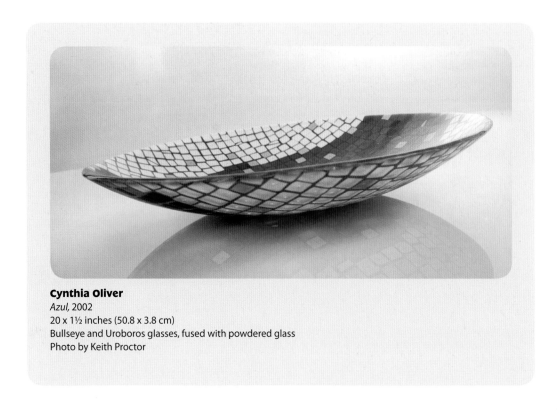

Cynthia Oliver
Azul, 2002
20 x 1½ inches (50.8 x 3.8 cm)
Bullseye and Uroboros glasses, fused with powdered glass
Photo by Keith Proctor

other materials. The most widely available and least-expensive release agent is kiln wash. Purchase the kind that's made for glass and either sprinkle it on as a powder, or mix it with water and apply it with a haik brush (see page 22).

Before applying kiln wash to a mullite shelf, you should first remove as much old kiln wash as possible. Everyone has his or her own preferred way to do this. I lift the kiln wash right off the shelf with a razor scraper, holding this tool at an angle of 30 to 35 degrees and pushing it across the shelf in long strokes, from edge to edge. This method cleanly removes the old kiln wash without generating much dust. You can also use an open-mesh grit cloth to sand off the kiln wash. To minimize the dust created by this removal method, wet the shelf first. Some kiln washes are labeled as removable with a damp sponge. I haven't tried them. No matter what removal method you use, make sure you wear your particulate respirator.

If you're combining kiln wash with water, mix them thoroughly. I brush the kiln wash across the entire surface in stripes, from edge to edge in one direction and then from edge to edge, perpendicular to the first layer. (You don't need to wait before applying the next coat.) For a normal temperature firing—up to 1500°F (816°C)—I use

When you apply kiln wash with a haik brush, you get better coverage and a smoother surface if you apply each coat perpendicular to the coat underneath it.

8 to 10 coats. For a high-temperature firing, such as a melt that goes up to 1650°F (899°C) and holds there for a while, I usually apply around 12 to 15 coats. Allow the shelf to dry completely before you place any glass on it.

If you use shelf paper or fiber paper between your glass and the kiln shelf, you won't need to apply any kiln wash.

TAKING A NEW KILN OUT FOR A SPIN

Getting your first kiln is both exciting and intimidating. Even though many new kilns come with computer controllers and preprogrammed firing schedules, you should take the time to learn how yours fires. If it's brand new, you'll probably need to do a break-in firing, as directed by the manufacturer. After that you should do a few test firings to find out how the basic firing schedules in this book work in your kiln. You may need to adjust final process temperatures and times to achieve the desired results.

The position of the kiln shelf inside the kiln will affect the outcome of any firing. A good rule of thumb is to position the shelf so that its top is level with the thermocouple for the kiln. The thermocouple measures the kiln temperature for the controller, so a shelf placed at the same height should have a surface temperature fairly close to the one read by the thermocouple. Because of their low thermal conductivity, ceramic boards and vermiculite shelves can be placed directly on the kiln floor. Because of their heat-retention properties, mullite should be placed on kiln posts to allow air circulation all around them.

Preparing Molds

Prepare ceramic and fiber-blanket molds just as you would mullite kiln shelves by using a haik brush to apply several coats of kiln wash. Most slump molds don't have much detail in them, but if your mold does, you may want to apply the kiln wash with an airbrush sprayer.

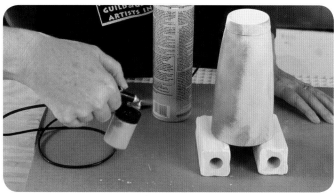

Using an airbrush to apply kiln wash to a heated metal mold creates a thin, even coat that won't run.

If the mold has vent holes in the bottom, after you've finished applying the wash, use the end of a paperclip to clean them out.

Metal molds take a little more effort to prepare than ceramic molds because kiln wash sticks better to rough, porous surfaces than to smooth metal ones. The best way to roughen the metal surface is to sandblast it, but sandpaper will also work. After roughening the surface, remove all the dust from the mold and heat the mold to 500°F (260°C) in the kiln. Use your silica-based gloves to remove the mold from the kiln and place it on a heat-resistant surface. Apply the kiln wash with a haik brush or with an airbrush sprayer; you'll achieve a much more even, dense covering with the sprayer. Brush or spray all exterior surfaces of the mold until they're completely and evenly coated. You may have to reheat the mold a few times and repeat the application of kiln wash to ensure good coverage.

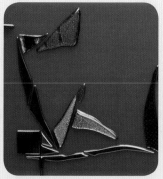

Robin Evans
Panta Rei (Everything Flows); Horizontal Grande Tower, 2006
32 x 14 x 6 inches (81.3 x 35.6 x 15.2 cm)
Multilayered fused glass in steel tower; dichroic glass accents; multiple firings
Photo by Grant Evans

Each time you remove a piece from the kiln, you'll need to decide if it's finished or if you want to do something more to it, either in the kiln or out. Everything you do to shape or work glass outside the kiln, without heat, is called "cold working." After fuse firings, for example, you may need to remove kiln wash stuck to the bottom of a piece, or you may want to grind a piece that's changed shape. If the piece will go back into the kiln for another fuse, you won't need to manually polish it after grinding; the heat of the kiln will do this for you. However, if all the firings are finished or the piece will only be slumped, you may want to polish it.

In addition to grinding or polishing, you may want to etch, sandblast, or glue your piece, or drill holes in it. In this section, you'll find a few tricks that will increase your chances of success with each of these activities.

Removing Kiln Wash

One of the most common cold-working tasks is removing kiln wash from the bottom of a piece. I used to struggle with this job, using kiln-wash remover and green nylon kitchen scrub pads—with limited success and swearing all the while. I even tried a razor scraper. Then I discovered how well 120-grit diamond hand pads work. (Remember, you always use water with these pads.)

Polishing

I find that if I've used a 120-grit diamond hand pad or bit on the edges of a piece, slumping takes the edge to at least a soft matte finish and sometimes all the way to a shine, depending on how soft the glass is. If I want to get back to a shiny, scratch-free edge on a slump, I use a 200-grit (or finer) pad or bit. If I plan to fire polish or fuse the piece, the heat alone will do the polishing for me, no matter how rough the edge is.

Polishing a piece to a high shine manually takes a lot of time and patience—and motorized equipment. I use a lap grinder; other artists sometimes prefer wet-belt sanders. No matter what tool you use, the principle of polishing remains the same: Start with the smallest grit number (the largest particle size); work to the largest grit number (finest particle size); and then use felt or cork with cerium oxide to finish. Belts and discs in 40 and 60 grit are great for removing large quantities of glass quickly, but you'll pay a price for the speed. Large grit and glass particles can gouge deep scratches in your piece and create big chips on its edges. If you try to jump right to 260 grit after using 60 grit, it will take forever to remove the scratches completely. If your discs are relatively new, start with a 100 grit instead and move gradually to finer grits.

Each time you change to a finer grit, you must polish away all the scratches and marks left by the previ-

A diamond hand pad, some water, and a little elbow grease do a great job of removing kiln wash from the back of a fired piece.

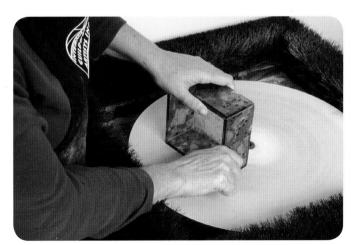

A lap grinder quickly polishes the flat surfaces of a fused piece and can also round off its edges.

ous grit. If you don't, you'll have an almost impossible time removing the scratches with an even finer grit. My current lap-grinder disc configuration is 100-, 180-, and 260-grit nickel-plated diamond discs, followed by 500- and 900-grit resin-bonded diamond pads, and finally, a white felt pad used with a cerium oxide slurry.

I mix in a jar a slurry of one part cerium oxide to two parts water, then pour the slurry sparingly onto the center of my flat lap grinder as it spins. I keep the felt pad wet (but not soaking) with my water feed, and as I polish, I periodically add a little more slurry. Polishing is a technique that takes some time to learn. You may not get it right the first time, but if you pay attention to what happens when you apply different amounts of water, cerium oxide, and pressure, you'll get better and faster at it.

The polishing technique you use will change depending on your equipment. Vertical lap grinders, wet-belt sanders, and handheld glass grinders/polishers require the use of thicker slurry (the consistency of mayonnaise), and the slurry should be applied to the glass rather than to the polishing pad.

Sandblasting

One way to change the entire surface of a piece is to sandblast it. Sandblasting is an easy, quick way to achieve a matte finish or to remove devitrification. The two materials most often used for sandblasting glass are aluminum oxide and silicon carbide. Both do an excellent job of etching and carving glass. Silicon carbide is harder, more expensive, and lasts longer, but it also can leave a filmy surface if you use it to sandblast a piece and then fuse another piece of glass on top of it. Many fusers report that aluminum oxide provides better final results. I find 120 to be the best overall grit size in either material.

Chemical Etching

Chemical etching will also produce a matte finish on the soda-lime glass used in fusing, but some glasses react better to the etching compound than others. If your glass still has shiny spots after etching, use a 200-grit diamond hand pad or fine sandpaper to scuff them lightly.

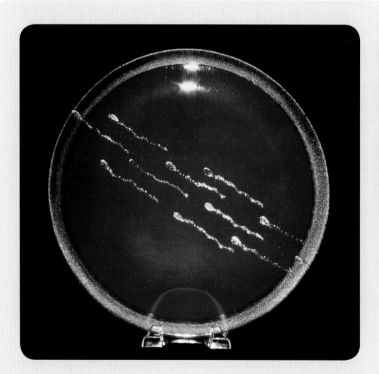
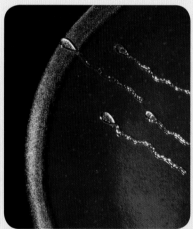

Robert Quarrick
One Out of Every…, 1996
14¼ x 14¼ x 1½ inches (36.2 x 36.2 x 3.8 cm)
Kiln-formed glass; flame-worked dichroic elements
Photo by artist

Using Adhesives

Several adhesives work well with glass, but no matter which one you use, you'll get the best results if you roughen the surface of the glass wherever you plan to apply the adhesive. Roughening the glass creates more surface area to which the adhesive can stick. I use my small, motorized grinding tool with a diamond bit, or my 100-grit diamond hand pads for this purpose.

Drilling Holes

Creating holes in glass is sometimes necessary; the Pop Art Fish Clock on page 84, for example, requires a hole for the clock mechanism. But drilling holes in glass isn't the same as drilling them in wood; instead, it involves grinding. Like all glass grinding, drilling is best done with a diamond bit that is kept wet. Use solid bits to grind small holes and core bits to make larger ones.

One way to keep your glass and diamond core drill bit wet as you drill a hole in glass is to construct a small, water-holding dam with modeling clay.

Barbara Galazzo
Jardin du Fantastique, 2005
56 x 17 x ½ inches (142.2 x 43.2 x 1.3 cm)
Cathedral, opal, dichroic glass; torch-pulled stems; fused, sawed, kiln carved, fire polished, cold worked
Photo by Allen Bryan

Core bits are much better than solid bits for creating large holes because they don't have to grind away as much glass—only enough to remove a glass circle.

A drill press isn't absolutely necessary, but drilling manually is risky because the bit can skip across the surface of your glass piece and ruin it. My bit manufacturer recommends core-drilling a hole by using a drill press run at speeds ranging from 125 to 800 rpm, depending on the diameter of the hole. As you drill, apply light pressure and watch for any discoloration at the tip of the bit. Discoloration indicates that the bit is overheating; this will shorten its life, and the heat can also cause your glass piece to break.

The simplest way to wet the hole as you drill is to submerge the glass completely in water. Place a block of wood under the area that you intend to drill and make sure that water covers the glass. If the piece is too large to immerse, support the glass on blocks of wood and use modeling clay to build a water-holding dam around the area you plan to drill. Fill the dammed area with water before drilling the hole. (To prevent chipping the back of the hole, I first drill slightly more than halfway through the glass. Then I turn the piece over, create a new dam, fill it with water, and drill the rest of the hole from the back.)

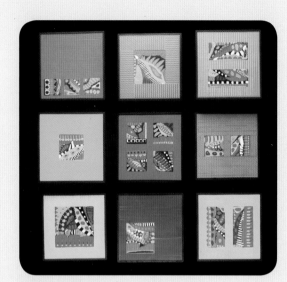

Jackie Beckman
Joseph's Pride, 2003
27½ x 27½ x 4 inches (69.9 x 69.9 x 10.2 cm)
Bullseye glass, kiln formed, carved, cold worked
Photo by artist

Barbara Galazzo
Boat – Collage Series, 2001
24 x 16 x 5 inches (61 x 40.6 x 12.7 cm)
Cathedral, opal glass; fused, sawed, kiln carved, slumped; extensive cold working
Photo by Allen Bryan

There are days when I open the kiln only to have my great expectations dashed by a huge, unexpected bubble in the middle of a piece or a crack right across its middle. Fortunately these days are fewer than they were when I started out. Much of what I know now, I learned through trial and error. Following are some of the common problems I've run across and some of their causes and cures.

Cracks and Breaks

You can often tell whether a break or crack in a piece happened as the kiln temperature was rising or falling. If it happened as the kiln was heating up, the edges of the crack will have been softened and rounded from the heat at the process temperature. Usually, these thermal-shock breaks occur when glass is heated too quickly. Sometimes, the glass will break spectacularly; the force will throw pieces to opposite sides of the kiln—always exciting! Thermal-shock breaks often look as if a pie had exploded into slices.

Another cause of cracking as the kiln heats up is stress that's present in the glass from a previous firing—either from incompatible glass or inadequate

Lesley C.S. Nolan
Sock Hop: Eric Wore His Favorite Shirt, 2006
20 x 27½ x 3 inches (50.8 x 69.9 x 7.6 cm)
Prefired, hand-decorated glass; pieced, fired, slumped
Photo by artist

annealing. If you're confident that the heating segments of your firing schedule were appropriately slow for the thickness of the glass you fired, and the firing during which cracking occurred wasn't the first firing of the piece, then the cause was probably poor annealing and/or incompatibility.

Incompatibility and poor annealing are also common causes of cracks and breaks that happen as glass cools. Compatibility isn't a permanent, static condition; glasses that are compatible can become incompatible after firing. One reason is that the different oxides used as colorants in glass can undergo chemical changes during long holds or multiple firings at high temperatures. If the chemical composition of the glass changes, the COE and viscosity of the glass can also change; these in turn affect its compatibility with other glasses.

Predicting which colors or glasses will undergo compatibility shifts and when they'll do so is impossible. One manufacturer's rule of thumb for preventing these shifts is never to subject the glass to more than three firings of 10 minutes each at 1500°F (816°C)—or

This bowl cracked because of thermal shock; it was heated too quickly during the slump firing.

to a cumulative time of more than 30 minutes at that temperature. Obviously, when you execute a melt, pour, or other high-temperature firing, you'll violate that guideline. Usually, these firings will work; sometimes they won't. If the break or crack seems to follow a de-marcation line between two different glasses, it's a safe bet that incompatibility was the culprit.

Bubbles

During fusing and other high-temperature processes, large bubbles can form in the glass. When air is trapped between the bottom of the glass and the kiln shelf, a big bubble can appear in the middle of your piece, usually because the ramp from 1250°F (677°C) to the full-process temperature was too fast. To help prevent bubbles, keep your ramp down to 400°F (204°C) per hour or slower; you can also use fiber paper between your piece

and the shelf to provide a way for the air to flow out.

Bubbles may also form in glass that's thinner than ¼ inch (6.4 mm). When I have to fire ¼-inch-wide (6.4 mm) strips to 1600°F (871°C), bubbles will often appear in the piece. I circumvent this problem by using ⅜-inch-wide (9.6 mm) strips instead.

Bubbles come in sizes other than large, and there's no way to eliminate them completely, but if you understand how they form and how they move through glass at higher temperatures, you can manage them. Gener-

Firing too quickly to the full process temperature can trap air under the piece and cause a large bubble.

To eliminate large bubbles, first puncture them with an awl. Then cover the craters with frit and fire the piece again.

Martin Kremer
Aventurine Trio, 2006
22 x 14 x 6 inches (55.9 x 35.6 x 15.2 cm)
Fused, kiln formed, sandblasted; stone base
Photo by Tommy Olaf Elder

ally, small bubbles aren't a problem in a finished piece unless they come to the surface and pop, leaving little craters in the surface that can potentially ruin the piece.

One way to avoid bubbles is by firing to a lower temperature and holding the glass there longer instead of firing all the way to 1500°F (816°C). I average 1450°F to 1465°F (788°C to 796°C), and I typically hold for 20 minutes or more.

To salvage a piece with a bubbled surface, use an awl to break any noticeable bubbles that have risen to the surface but that haven't broken. Then overlap or fill the holes with frit in clear or matching colors, and fire the piece to full fuse again. Try to avoid covering the holes completely with frit, as doing so may trap air and create another bubble. One caution when using this method with colored frit: I've found differences in color between sheets of glass and frit from the same manufacturer (much as the colors of paint and dye lots sometimes differ); these differences can be severe enough to make your frit mending very visible.

Devitrification

As glass cools after it's been heated to melting temperature, the silica in it can sometimes reform into crystals—a process known as devitrification. Some glasses seem to devitrify more than others. One cause is a contaminant on the surface of the glass; make sure your glass is clean before you fire it.

You can sometimes repair a devitrified piece. Some people like to remove the old surface of the glass and expose a new one by sandblasting the glass. However, if you don't clean the glass well enough after sandblasting, the sandblasting compound (aluminum oxide or silicon carbide) can contaminate the surface and cause devitrification to recur.

An overspray can be used to repair devitrification as well as prevent it (see page 52). For repair work, I've had very good success with the following procedure. First I use my diamond hand pads to remove any large,

Diane Anderson
Untitled, 2006
6 x 20 x ⅝ inches (15.2 x 50.8 x 1.6 cm)
Transparent frits, kiln cast, slumped, hand finished
Photo by artist

bumpy surface areas that devitrified and didn't melt evenly into the base. Then I clean the piece thoroughly and apply multiple thin, even coats of overspray with my airbrush sprayer. Finally, I refire the piece to 1425°F (774°C), with no hold at the top temperature. I cool and anneal with my basic fusing schedule.

Hazing

Another problem I frequently encounter is a milky-white haze on the bottom of opal glass pieces if I used shelf paper when I fused them. I've had some limited success preventing this haze by venting the kiln 1 inch (2.5 cm) on the initial rise to 1000°F (538°C); this allows the binders in the paper to burn off. Sandblasting is the only other way I've been able to remove the haze completely.

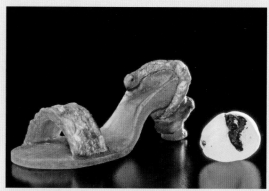

Delores Taylor
Wicket Fit, 2004
2 x 3 x 6 inches (5.1 x 7.6 x 15.2 cm)
Pâte de verre; kiln cast
Photo by Roger Schrieber

Jackie Beckman
Saturday at the Rocks, 2005
19 x 40 x 3 inches (48.3 x 101.6 x 7.6 cm)
Bulllseye glass, kiln formed, cold worked
Photo by artist

Now that you're familiar with the basics, it's time to try your hand at the real thing—and have some real fun. In the pages that follow, you'll find a wonderful range of beautiful projects, all made with Tested Compatible glass and all accompanied by clear, step-by-step instructions. Each set of project instructions comes with a list of the tools and materials you'll need, as well as useful how-to photographs; some also include special firing schedules, illustrations, and useful tips. Several projects require templates to help you cut the required glass shapes; these are included in a special section (see pages 122–25).

Start by browsing through the projects and selecting one that appeals to you. The instructions for them are presented in order of complexity, from easiest to most challenging, so you'll get plenty of useful practice if you start with the first and work your way through to the last. If you'd rather start with one in the middle, go right ahead. Each project teaches a different technique, from simple slumping and draping to casting and pâte de verre, so no matter where you begin, you'll learn something new. Even experienced kiln formers will find valuable tips and techniques within this section.

Once you've chosen a project, read through the instructions carefully. Next, gather the tools and materials that you need in order to create it. Then as you work, relax; you'll have much more fun if you do. Enjoy your foray into the fascinating world of creating kiln-formed glass.

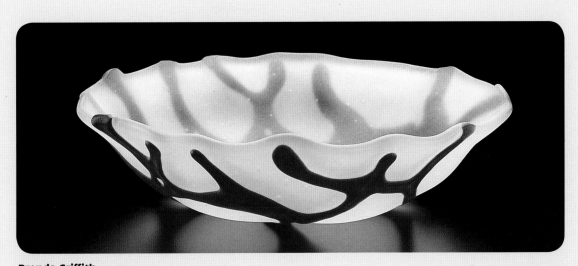

Brenda Griffith
Cailleach's Cradle, 2006
12 x 3 inches (30.5 x 7.6 cm)
Bullseye glass; slumped and sandblast etched; cast lace fused to bowl
Photo by Keith Proctor

FLORAL VASE AND VOTIVE

Though this lovely vase and votive candle holder can each be made with one piece of draped glass, the most beautiful results come from using an outer layer of either opaque or transparent patterned glass and a complementary transparent glass for the inside layer.

TOOLS AND MATERIALS

2 pieces of contrasting glass, each 10 x 15 inches (25.4 x 38.1 cm)

1 or 2 metal floral drape molds, 3 inches (6.4 cm) in diameter and 7 inches (17.8 cm) in height (second mold optional)

Basic Tools and Supplies (see page 16)

Shelf paper, 10 inches square (25.4 cm)

4 pieces of mullite, each ½ x 1 x 1 inch (1.3 x 2.5 x 2.5 cm)

Airbrush sprayer (optional)

INSTRUCTIONS

Note: To help you use your glass stock most efficiently, the instructions tell how to make two votives instead of just one.

1 Prepare the metal mold with kiln wash (see page 54).

2 Cut each piece of glass into two 5-inch (12.7 cm) squares and one 10-inch (25.4 cm) square.

3 Using a 220-grit diamond hand pad, smooth the edges and corners of each piece of glass until they're slightly rounded and no longer sharp.

4 Wash and dry all the glass.

5 To prevent any glass that drapes that far from sticking to the bottom of the kiln, place the shelf paper in the middle of the kiln floor.

ESSENTIAL TIP

Because the votive pieces are smaller than the pieces for the vase, they won't drape as fully if you use the same firing schedule as you do for the vase. To achieve a more pronounced drop for the votive, you'll extend the firing just a bit.

6 Place the mulite pieces on the paper, then set the mold on top of them, with its opening face down. Center one 10-inch (25.4 cm) square of glass on top of the mold.

7 Place the second 10-inch (25.4 cm) square of glass on top of the first piece, with its corners extending out over the sides of the first piece (see photo).

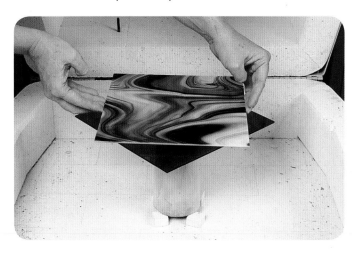

8 Fire the glass, using the Basic Slump Schedule (see page 48).

9 When the kiln is cool, remove the vase. You don't need to prepare the metal mold again unless it has any bare areas or any glass stuck to it from the first firing.

10 To make the first votive, lay out two 5-inch (12.7 cm) squares of glass on the mold, just as you did for the vase. (If you have a second mold, arrange the remaining glass on it for the second votive.)

11 Fire the glass, using the Basic Slump Schedule (see page 48), but add 10 minutes to the hold time at the top temperature.

12 If you have only one mold, repeat steps 10 and 11 to make the second votive.

FAUX-WEAVE LATTICE PLATE

Remember Grandma's beautiful apple-pie crust? This wonderfully evocative slumped plate — strong enough to serve as the base of a table centerpiece — is made with two layers of glass strips cut from a single circle of glass.

TOOLS AND MATERIALS

Cobalt transparent iridescent glass, 13 inches square (33 cm)

Round plate mold, 1 inch (2.5 cm) deep and 12 inches (30.5 cm) in diameter

Basic Tools and Supplies (see page 16)

INSTRUCTIONS

1 If your mold is new, prepare it with kiln wash and let it dry completely.

2 Cut a 12-inch (30.5 cm) circle from the middle of the cobalt glass.

3 Score parallel lines across the glass circle, ¼ to 1¼ inches (6.4 mm to 31.8 cm) apart.

4 Using your breaking pliers, gently snap the scored glass into strips, arranging them on your work surface in the same order that you cut them. If a strip breaks into two or three pieces, save the pieces and continue to snap the rest of the strips. If a strip breaks into more than three pieces, set it aside; you won't use it for this project.

5 Continuing to keep the strips in order, use a 220-grit diamond hand pad to smooth any bumps off their edges and ends, wash and dry them, and place them back on the work surface.

6 Arrange the strips so that every other one sticks up higher than its neighbors (photo 1). Any broken strips should be in one group of strips or the other—not in both. If there are broken pieces in both groups, try to move them into a single group by switching pieces of similar sizes and end shapes. You'll use the group of unbroken pieces to make up the bottom layer of the plate.

1

7 Place the centermost strip from the bottom-layer group across the mold, near its center so that its ends line up with the edges of the mold. Lay out the remaining strips for the bottom layer. Make sure they're parallel and that their ends line up with the rim of the mold. If broken strips that couldn't be switched remain in this group, either cut new strips to replace them, or—if their absence won't leave very wide gaps—leave them out completely.

8 To clean up the ends of any broken pieces in the top-layer group, trim each broken end at a 45-degree angle to the long edge (photo 2) to create a ½ to 1-inch-wide (1.3 to 2.5 cm) gap between the angled ends. If you have no broken pieces or would like to add more for visual interest, cut three to five of the strips at 45-degree angles to their long edges. Then cut each one again, parallel to the original cut, to create a ½ to 1-inch-wide (1.3 to 2.5 cm) gap between the two sections of each strip. Clean the edges of the newly cut pieces. Carefully choosing which strips to cut can add interesting variations to your plate (photo 3).

9 Beginning with the centermost intact strip in this group, position the strips across the mold, perpendicular to the bottom-layer strips, aligning their ends with the rim of the mold. When you come to a cut strip, first position the intact strips that it will rest between. (Because of their lengths, the intact strips must be placed in specific positions so that their curved ends will line up with rim of the mold.) Then position the broken strip between them, lining up its ends with the rim of the mold, as well.

10 Fire the piece, using the Basic Slump Schedule (see page 48).

HARLEQUIN CANDLE TRAYS

This ingenious design is made by cutting the same pattern from two different glass sheets, then switching half of the pieces. Fibrous silica shelf cloth gives the glass its unusual texture.

TOOLS AND MATERIALS

Coral transparent glass, 7 x 12 inches (17.8 x 30.5 cm)

Clear glass with black stringer, 7 x 12 inches (17.8 x 30.5 cm)

2 pieces of peach opal glass, each 7 x 12 inches (17.8 x 30.5 cm)

Basic Tools and Supplies (see page 16)

Fibrous silica shelf cloth, 9 x 14 inches (22.9 x 35.6 cm)

Rectangular mold, 7 x 12 inches (17.8 x 30.5 cm)

Strip-cutting system (optional)

INSTRUCTIONS

1 Prefire the piece of fibrous silica shelf cloth (see Essential Tips).

2 If your mold is new, prepare it with kiln wash and let it dry completely.

3 Using a fine-tipped black permanent marker, transfer the Harlequin Candle Tray template (see page 122) and its interior design lines to the coral glass and to the clear stringer glass, as well. (You'll cut 18 pieces for the two trays—nine from each piece of glass.)

4 Score on the drawn lines, using a handheld cutter and straightedge, or a strip-cutting system. Then use your breaking pliers to break both rectangles into pieces along the score lines.

ESSENTIAL TIPS

- **You'll be cutting enough pieces for two trays, so it's more efficient to make them both; the pattern on each will be a mirror image of the other.**

- **The trick to making these trays is to score all the lines on the rectangles before breaking them.**

- **Shelf cloth shrinks by about five percent the first time you fire it, so it should be prefired, using the following schedule: 500°F (277°C)/hour to 1400°F (760°C), hold 10 minutes, and cool naturally to room temperature.**

5 Wash and dry all the glass.

6 On your work surface, assemble the cut pieces into two new rectangles by switching the even-numbered pieces in the coral rectangle with the even-numbered pieces in the clear stringer rectangle.

7 Place the fibrous silica shelf cloth on the kiln shelf, positioning the weave you'd like to use for your piece face up so its texture will be transferred to the glass.

8 Lay out one of the reassembled rectangles face down on the cloth (see photo). Place an uncut peach opal rectangle on top of the assembled pieces. Make sure all the glass edges line up evenly.

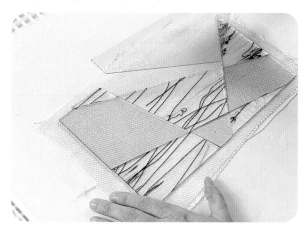

9 Fire the glass, using the Basic Fuse Schedule (see page 50).

10 Let the piece cool completely before removing it from the shelf cloth. If you remove it too soon, you may tear or otherwise damage the cloth.

11 Wash the fired piece and use a plastic scrub brush to remove any residue from the shelf cloth.

12 Place the fired piece on the mold, textured side up, and fire it, using the Basic Slump Schedule (see page 48). When the piece is completely cool, remove it from the kiln.

13 Repeat steps 7 through 12 to create the second tray.

IRIDESCENT PENDANT

Simple and gracefully shaped, this pendant's eye-catching, multilevel effect is created with simple fusing techniques.

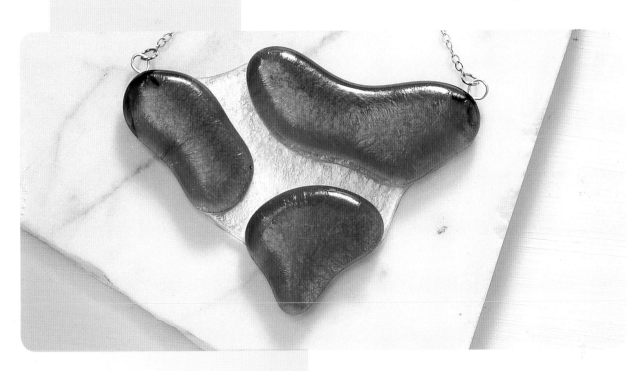

TOOLS AND MATERIALS

Amber iridescent transparent glass, 4 inches square (10.2 cm)

Amber glass, 4 inches square (10.2 cm)

Thin clear iridescent glass, ¹⁄₁₆-inch (1.6 mm) thick and 5 inches square (12.7 cm)

Basic Tools and Supplies (see page 16)

Paper for patterns

2 inches (5.1 cm) of 20-gauge sterling silver wire

Jeweler's pliers

Round-nose pliers

Wire cutters

2 pieces of fiber paper, ¹⁄₁₆ x ¼ x ½ inch (1.6 mm x 6.4 mm x 1.3 cm)

Silver chain, 18 inches (45.7 cm) long

4 silver jump rings, 4 mm size

Silver necklace clasp

INSTRUCTIONS

1 Using the Iridescent Pendant template (see page 122), draw and cut out paper patterns for each of the three amber pieces.

2 Trace the three patterns onto the iridescent surface of the amber glass, using a fine-tipped black permanent marker.

3 Score each piece, running your cutter along the outside edges of the marker lines. Break out the three pieces, then wash and dry them.

4 Trace the same three patterns onto the 4-inch-square (10.2 cm) amber glass. This time, score along the inner edges of the pattern lines. The slightly larger pieces of amber iridescent glass will serve to cap the amber pieces and will give the pendant a finished look. Break these pieces out, then wash and dry them.

5 Lay the amber pieces on a prepared kiln shelf, at least ½ inch (1.3 cm) apart. Position a matching amber iridescent piece on top of each one, iridescent side up.

6 Fuse the glass, using the Basic Small-Object Fuse Schedule on this page.

7 When the pieces are cool, remove them from the kiln. Prepare the kiln shelf again.

8 To make the pendant base, place the thin iridescent clear glass in front of you, with the noniridescent side up, and arrange the amber pieces on it. Then use the marker to trace a shape defined by their outer edges (see photo). (If you like, you can center the thin iridescent glass over the Iridescent Pendant template to view the basic placement of the amber pieces before you trace them.) Score on the marked line, break out this base piece, and wash and dry it.

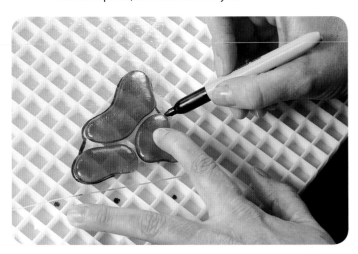

9 Using the silver wire, make two loops (figure 1) by using the jeweler's pliers to bend them around the end of the round-nose pliers. Cut the wire with the wire cutters.

Figure 1

10 Place the glass base on the kiln shelf, iridescent side down (the amber glass won't adhere well if it's tack fused to the iridescent surface). The two small pieces of fiber paper will support the outer portions of the silver loops at the same height as the base glass. Place one piece at each upper corner of the base glass, and position each loop so it rests on both the base glass and a piece of fiber paper, with its twisted ends on the glass. Arrange the fused amber pieces on top of the base so the twisted loop ends are sandwiched between them and the base.

11 Fire the pendant, using the Basic Tack-Fuse Schedule (see page 50), but add 10 minutes to the top hold time (H1) to allow for incorporation of the silver rings.

12 When the pendant is cool, remove it from the kiln. If the silver loops have oxidized, polish them with a small piece of steel wool.

13 Cut the silver chain in half with the wire cutters. Fasten a silver jump ring to each of the loops on the necklace and a length of chain to each ring. Try on the necklace to determine the desired length. A standard chain is 16 inches (40.6 cm) long, so if you plan to give the necklace away and can't measure the length on the recipient, cut each chain length to 8 inches (20.3 cm). Using the remaining jump rings, attach the silver necklace clasp sections to the free ends of the chain lengths.

BASIC SMALL-OBJECT FUSE SCHEDULE

STAGE	FAHRENHEIT / CELSIUS
R1	600°F (333°C)/hour
L1	1465°F (796°C)
H1	15 minutes
R2	AFAP
L2	960°F (516°C)
H2	30 minutes

SEA-GLASS WIND CHIMES

The delicate music of these etched chimes may bring to mind the childhood pleasure of hunting for "sea glass" — those bits of broken bottles washed clean and sanded smooth by the ocean.

TOOLS AND MATERIALS

12 pieces of pale green transparent glass, each 1 x 6 inches (2.5 x 15.2 cm)

12 pieces of purple transparent glass, each 1 inch square (2.5 cm)

3 pieces of clear glass rod, each 7⅞ inches long (22.8 cm)

Basic Tools and Supplies (see page 16)

12 inches (30.5 cm) of 18-gauge copper wire

Rounded ballpoint pen or similar tubular object

Wire cutters

Needle-nose pliers

Fiber paper, ⅛ x 1 x 8 inches (3.2 mm x 2.5 cm x 20.3 cm)

Glass-etching solution and applicator (paintbrush or cotton swab)

30 silver crimp beads

15-pound test monofilament line

INSTRUCTIONS

Making the Chimes

1 Using the copper wire, ballpoint pen, and wire cutters, make at least 15 copper rings. First, wrap some wire several times around any tubular object; a ballpoint pen works well (photo 1). Slip the coiled wire off and use wire cutters to clip a straight line through the coils, which will separate them into individual rings (photo 2).

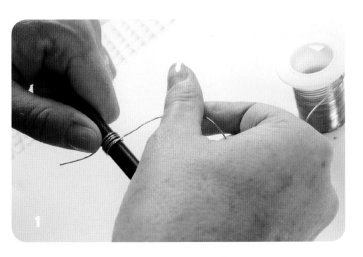

2 Use the needle-nose pliers to flatten the ends of each ring where the cut ends meet.

3 Wash and dry all the glass.

4 Place the strip of fiber paper across the middle of a prepared kiln shelf. Then line up a row of six pieces of the green glass along the bottom edge of the strip so they almost touch it.

5 Set a copper ring on top of each piece of green glass so the split portion of the ring rests on the glass and the solid portion rests on the fiber paper.

6 Position another piece of green glass on top of each of the six pieces already in place, being careful not to dislodge the rings. Each ring should be securely sandwiched between two pieces of glass (photo 3).

7 Arrange six purple squares above the strip of fiber paper, with their bottom corners almost touching it. Then repeat steps 5 and 6 to set a copper ring at the bottom corner of each square and sandwich each ring by placing another purple square on top.

8 Fire the glass, using the Basic Fuse Schedule (see page 50).

9 When the kiln is cool, remove the fused chimes. Clean them thoroughly and brush the copper rings to a shine with fine steel wool.

10 Following the manufacturer's instructions, etch the green chimes and the three clear rods with the glass-etching solution; keep in mind that some glasses are more easily etched with chemicals than others. After etching, use fine-grit sandpaper to roughen any remaining shiny spots. Repeated applications may be necessary to achieve the desired results. Sandblasting works well for etching any glass (see page 56).

Assembling the Chimes

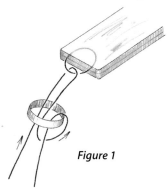

Figure 1

11 Thread a silver crimp bead onto the monofilament line, but don't cut the line from the spool yet. Run the line through the ring on one of the chimes and back through the bead (figure 1). Then loop the line around the bead and snug the bead up to the ring. Squeeze the bead closed with the needle-nose pliers.

12 Cut the tail of the line close to the bead. Then cut the line from the spool, 12 inches (30.5 cm) from the bead.

13 Repeat steps 11 and 12 to thread the rest of the chimes.

14 The green pieces hang from one glass rod, and the purple ones hang from another. The third glass rod provides strength and stability, and holds the first two rods in place. Marking the lines and rods before assembly will help the chimes to hang correctly. Using a black permanent marker, mark each of the green-glass lines 5¼ inches (14.6 cm) from the top of the crimp bead.

15 Make two pencil marks on one of the rods, 1 inch (2.5 cm) from each end. Then make a mark every 1⅛ inches (2.9 cm) between the two 1-inch (2.5 cm) marks. Repeat to make the same marks on one of the other rods.

16 Thread a bead onto one of the green-glass lines. Wrap the tail end of the line twice around one of the marked rods so the mark on the line is just below the mark on the rod. Run the line back through the bead, and loop the line through it. Snug the bead up against the rod and squeeze it closed with the pliers. Repeat with the other green chimes. Cut off all the line tails close to the beads.

17 The purple chimes in this project are hung at different lengths. Mark two of the purple-chime lines 9¼ inches (23.5 cm) from the top of the bead; two at 7½ inches (19.1 cm); and two at 6¼ inches (15.9 cm).

18 Repeat step 16 to hang the purple chimes from the second marked rod in this order: long, medium, short, long, medium, and short.

19 Mark the third rod ½ inch (1.3 cm) in from each end. Hold the first two rods together, with their lengths pressed against each other, so the chimes hang freely beneath them. Place the third rod on top to form a long bundle.

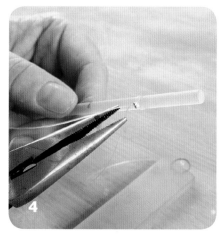

20 Unwind some line from the spool and thread a bead onto it, about 3 inches (7.6 cm) from the end. Hold the bead on top of the rods, over one of the two marks on the third rod. Wrap the tail of line coming out of the bead tightly around the bundled rods three times. Run the tail of the line back through the bead. Then loop it around the bead, snug the bead tight against the top of the rods, and squeeze the bead closed with the pliers (photo 4).

21 Mark the line 18 inches (45.7 cm) from the top of the bead. Then cut the line 3 inches (7.6 cm) past that mark and thread a bead onto it. Wrap and crimp this end of the line at the second mark on the third rod, as in step 20. Cut the tails close to the beads.

Paperweights can be fun as well as functional. Make these cheery dragonflies by casting frit in a commercial slip mold.

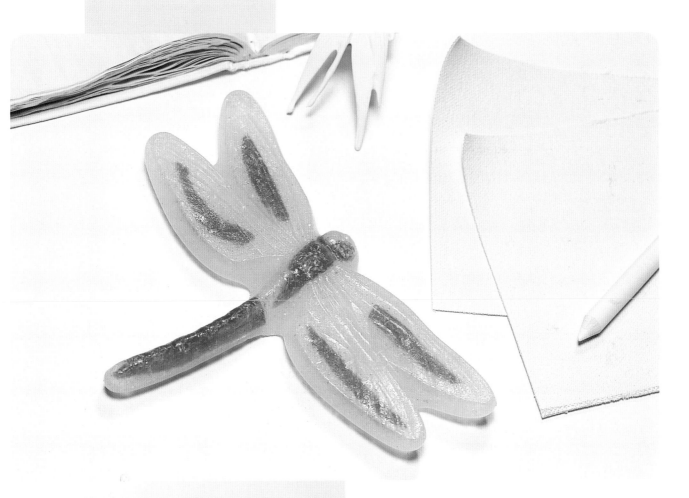

TOOLS AND MATERIALS

Two commercial slip molds for glass casting

Enough frit to fill the molds

Basic Tools and Supplies (see page 16)

Airbrush sprayer (optional)

Make-up spatula (optional)

INSTRUCTIONS

note: Be sure to read the essential tips on page 78.

1 If your molds are new, prepare them with kiln wash. The best way to do this is to first apply a light coat to the entire surface with an airbrush, which doesn't obscure fine details as a brush would. Then heat the molds in the kiln to 500°F (260°C). While they are still hot, slowly apply several more coats of kiln wash. The heat evaporates the water in the kiln wash before it has time to run down the molds and ruin their design details. Let the molds dry completely before you fill them with frit.

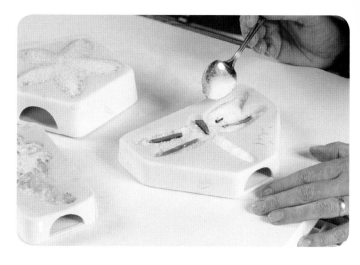

- The size of your frit will affect the size and appearance of your casting. You might think that very fine-grained frit would result in a larger, more transparent piece, but in fact, the finer the frit, the more air bubbles will be trapped in the piece, and the more opaque the finished casting will look. Mixing different sizes of frit in the mold is the most efficient way to minimize shrinkage.

- There are different ways to fill molds with frit than the one presented here. If you're feeling exuberant, mix all your colors together and just pour the frit into the molds. For maximum control, mix each color with fuser's glue to make a paste that holds together without crumbling, then use a make-up spatula to pack it into the appropriate area of each mold.

- The glass you choose and how you layer it can provide interesting effects. Transparent and opal glasses transmit and reflect light differently. The most important thing to remember about color is that less is more. It takes very little of a medium-colored transparent glass, for example, to create a strong, dark color. Some glass manufacturers make what they call *tints*—colors so pale that in single-sheet thicknesses, they look almost clear. Tints were made to give rich, vibrant color to thick castings. Opal colors appear much the same before firing as they do in the fired casting because opal glass primarily reflects light rather than transmitting it.

2 Use a spoon to fill the molds with frit, arranging the colors wherever you like (photo 1). Pile the frit higher in the middle than around the sides. As the glass melts and sinks into the molds, it should push the glass around the edges upward, rounding them gently. Frit that's piled high on the sides will fall instead of rising and can leave sharp, needlelike points along the top edges of the castings.

3 Fire the pieces, using the schedule that comes with your commercial molds or the Basic Slip-Mold Cast Schedule on this page.

4 When the molds are completely cool, take them out of the kiln and carefully turn them over. Your cast pieces will fall right out. Remove any rough edges with your diamond hand pads.

BASIC SLIP-MOLD CAST SCHEDULE

STAGE	FAHRENHEIT / CELSIUS
R1	600°F (333°C)/hour
L1	1450°F (788°C)
H1	30 minutes
R2	AFAP
L2	960°F (516°C)
H2	90 minutes
R3	100°F (56°C)/hour
L3	700°F (371°C)
H3	off

CONFETTI AND STREAMERS CANDY DISH

Once your guests have eaten the goodies on this beautiful plate, they'll find the real treats — confetti and streamer designs, created with mica powders — sandwiched between two layers of glass.

TOOLS AND MATERIALS

Clear glass, 8¼ inches square (21 cm)

*Light blue, transparent iridescent glass,
    8 inches square (20.3 cm)*

Mica powders, silver and gold

Basic Tools and Supplies (see page 16)

Adhesive shelf paper, 8¼ inches square (21 cm)

*3 soft, natural-bristle paintbrushes,
    with ¼-inch-wide (6.4 mm) tips*

Gum arabic

Round dish mold, 7½ inches (19.1 cm) in diameter

INSTRUCTIONS

1 Cut a 7¾-inch-diameter (19.7 cm) circle from the clear glass and a 7½-inch-diameter (19.1 cm) circle from the light blue glass.

2 Wash and dry the glass circles.

3 Peel the backing off the adhesive shelf paper and apply it to the noniridescent surface of the blue glass. Use a craft knife to trim any excess from around the edges.

4 Using the craft knife, cut a series of random ½ to ¾-inch (1.3 to 1.9 cm) squares from the adhesive paper, leaving room around them to cut smaller squares and streamer shapes. Cut ¼-inch (6.4 mm) squares to mingle in with the larger squares; then cut curling streamer shapes around the squares.

5 Peel the large squares of adhesive paper off the glass, but leave the small squares and streamers in place.

6 Use one paintbrush to cover all the exposed squares of glass with gum arabic. Sprinkle silver mica lightly over these squares and work it into the gum arabic by pouncing another paintbrush down into the powder. Try to keep the mica brush dry for applying more mica. Load more mica onto it by dabbing it repeatedly into the mica until it is full. You can brush the mica into the gum arabic with a wet brush, but I like the texture and

consistency I get from pouncing with a dry one. Add more gum arabic and more mica as necessary to cover all the squares well and evenly. Rinse the gum arabic brush thoroughly and gently squeeze it dry.

7 Peel the adhesive paper off the small squares and streamers.

8 Repeat step 6, using the third paintbrush and gold mica to fill in the small squares and streamers (photo 1).

9 Carefully peel away the remaining adhesive paper from the blue glass. Place the glass on a prepared kiln shelf, mica side up, and cover it with the clear glass circle. (This circle is slightly larger than the blue glass circle for a specific reason. Mica doesn't melt during fusing. If the circles were the same size and there were any mica between them at their edges, the glass circles wouldn't be able to fuse together. The larger circle used here caps the base and prevents gaps around the edges of the fused piece.)

10 Fire the glass, using the Basic Fuse Schedule (see page 50).

11 If your round dish mold is new, prepare it with kiln wash and let it dry completely.

12 When the fused glass is cool, place it on the mold and fire it, using the Basic Slump Schedule (see page 48).

PÂTE DE VERRE SUGAR SQUARE

Bright, vibrant colors and crisp geometric shapes make this pâte de verre piece a delight to behold. Mixing fuser's glue with the frit makes placement of the different colors a snap.

TOOLS AND MATERIALS

¼ pound (113 g) each of fine opal frit in lime green, yellow, orange, and blue

½ pound (227 g) each of fine opal frit in red and black

Slump mold, 10 inches square (25.4 cm)

Fuser's glue

Basic Tools and Supplies (see page 16)

Make-up spatula (optional)

Paperclip with one end bent open

Small, soft paintbrush with a fluffy end

INSTRUCTIONS

1 If your mold is new, prepare it with kiln wash and let it dry completely.

2 With a pencil and a ruler, draw the pattern shown in the Pâte de Verre Sugar Square template (see page 123) onto the mold.

3 Mix some of the lime-green frit with enough fuser's glue to hold the mixture together in a ball that doesn't flake.

4 Use a spoon or the make-up spatula to transfer the mixture to the appropriate area of the mold. Using your fingers, press the mixture down firmly into a ³⁄₁₆-inch-thick (4.8 mm) layer (photo 1). Line up the straight edges with the edge of the spatula or a straightedge. To check the depth of the frit layer, make a gauge by wrapping a small piece of masking tape around the opened end of the paperclip, leaving ³⁄₁₆ inch (4.8 mm)

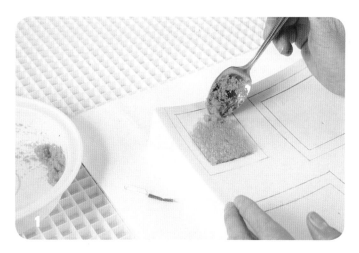

of the pointed end exposed. Push the taped end of the paperclip straight down into the frit layer until it touches the mold; the top of the frit layer should just reach the bottom of the masking tape. Adjust the frit depth as necessary.

5 Repeat steps 3 and 4 with the yellow, orange, and blue frits. If you accidentally drop bits of one color onto an area of another color, remove them by dabbing them lightly with the dry paintbrush.

6 The black outlines are best completed in small sections. Rather than dumping a lot of the frit-and-glue mixture down at one time, position small mounds of it with your spoon or spatula, and press them into place. Continue to check the frit depth and evenness as you work.

7 When you've outlined all the squares and rectangles in black, fill in the remaining areas with a red frit-and-glue mixture. Complete a final depth check and look carefully over the surface to make sure it's uniformly flat. Unlike other fused pieces that flatten out and flow together as the glass melts, this one will come out of the kiln looking exactly the same as it did going in; any flaws it starts out with will remain in the finished project.

8 Fire the piece, using the Basic Tack-Fuse Schedule (see page 50).

POP ART FISH CLOCK

The bright, modern design makes this clock a real conversation piece. Layering a transparent glass circle on top of an opal one makes the small circles look as if they're floating.

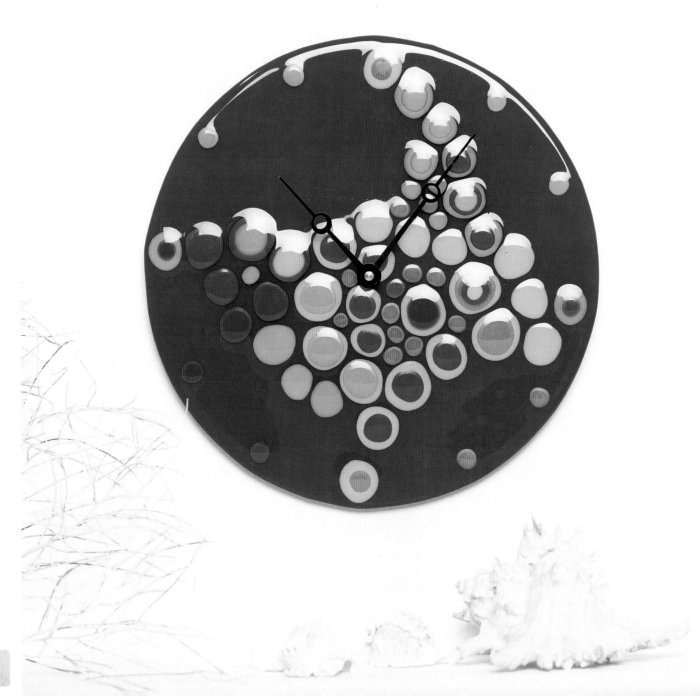

INSTRUCTIONS

1 Cut a 12-inch-diameter (30.5 cm) circle from each of the red pieces of glass.

2 Cut all the 4-inch (10.2 cm) glass squares and some of the red opal scrap left from the large circle into circles ranging from ⅜ to 1¼ inches (1 to 3.2 cm) in diameter (see Essential Tip). Most of these circles should be from ¾ to 1 inch (1.9 to 2.5 cm) in diameter.

3 Wash and dry all the circles.

4 Place the large red opal circle in the middle of a prepared kiln shelf and set the red transparent circle on top of it.

5 Design your clock face by arranging the small glass circles (photo 1).

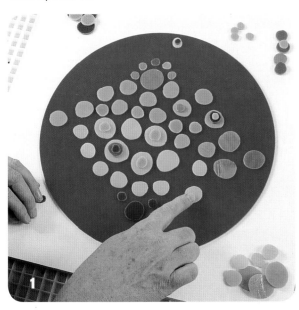

6 When you're satisfied with your layout, the piece is ready to be fused, but you may want to apply a coat of overspray first, as opal glasses often devitrify (see pages 52 and 61–62 for information on devitrification). If you want to use an overspray, apply it now.

TOOLS AND MATERIALS

Red opal glass, 14 inches square (35.6 cm)

Red transparent glass, 14 inches square (35.6 cm)

5 pieces of opal glass (yellow, orange, blue, turquoise, and lime green), each 4 inches square (10.2 cm)

Basic Tools and Supplies (see page 16)

Large circle cutter (optional)

Ring saw or small circle cutter (optional)

Overspray (optional)

Clock mechanism, hands, and battery

Airbrush sprayer (optional)

Diamond core drill bit, ⁵⁄₁₆ inch (7.9 mm) larger in diameter than that of the clock's post (optional)

Drill press (optional)

Modeling clay (optional)

7 Place the shelf in the kiln and fire the glass, using the Basic Fuse Schedule (see page 50).

8 When the piece is completely cool, use the diamond core drill bit to drill a hole through its center, or have someone do this for you. For instructions on drilling holes in glass, see pages 57–58.

9 Clean the fused piece, insert the mechanism post through the drilled hole, and attach the hands.

ESSENTIAL TIP

The small circles for this project are meant to be cut freehand so they'll look organic and less than perfect in shape. A ring saw is the ideal tool for this job, but a handheld cutter or a small circle cutter will also work

OPEN POCKET VASE

A pocket vase makes a wonderful gift, but this one's so pretty that once you've made it, you may not want to give it away. The front of the pocket is fused to the back so it can hold water for fresh flowers.

TOOLS AND MATERIALS

Transparent cobalt blue glass, 5 inches square (12.7 cm)

Patterned yellow, cobalt-blue, and clear glass, 5½ x 6¼ inches (14 x 15.9 cm)

Transparent cobalt-blue glass, 5 x 6 inches (12.7 x 15.2 cm)

Basic Tools and Supplies (see page 16)

Paper for pattern

4 inches (10.2 cm) of 18-gauge copper wire

Permanent marker or any tubular object roughly ½ inch (1.3 cm) in diameter

Wire cutters

3 pieces of fiber paper, each ⅛ x 4 x 5½ inches (3.2 mm x 10.2 cm x 14 cm)

2 pieces of fiber paper, each ⅛ x ½ x ½ inch (3.2 mm x 1.3 cm x 1.3 cm)

Needle-nose pliers

Copper chain, 12 inches (30.5 cm) long

INSTRUCTIONS

1 Make a paper pattern from the Open Pocket Vase template (see page124) and use a black permanent marker to transfer the design to the 5-inch square (12.7 cm) of cobalt-blue glass. Score and break out this piece.

2 Wash and dry all the glass.

3 To make a double-looped copper ring, wrap the copper wire tightly around the shaft of the marker twice. Slip the doubled coil off the marker and use the wire cutters to cut the wire so the ends of the two-loop ring meet each other. Repeat to make a second two-loop ring.

4 Place the 5 x 6-inch (12.7 x 15.2 cm) blue glass in the center of a prepared kiln shelf, with its long edges at the sides and its short edges at the top and bottom; this piece will form the back of the vase.

5 Refer to photo 1; it will help you with the next several steps.

6 Stack the three large pieces of fiber paper. Place the stack on the blue glass base, lining up its front edge evenly with the front edge of the base and centering it between the long edges of the base.

7 Place the small squares of fiber paper at the sides of the base glass to serve as supports for the copper rings. Position these squares ¼ inch (6.4 mm) away from the sides of the glass.

8 Set a double-looped copper ring on each fiber-paper square and on the glass so the ring bridges the gap between the square and glass. About one-third to one-half of each ring—and its cut ends—should rest on the glass.

9 Place the patterned glass on top of the fiber-paper stack so that one 5½-inch-long (14 cm) edge is even with the front edge of the stack and centered over it.

10 Place the pattern-cut glass piece on top of the patterned glass, with its straight edge overlapping the stack-supported edge of the patterned glass by just a little bit. This tiny overlap will allow the pattern-cut piece to roll over the edge of the patterned glass and create a smooth edge as it fuses.

11 Fire the glass, using the Basic Pocket-Vase Fuse Schedule on this page.

12 When the piece is cool, remove the fiber paper by scooping it out with a pencil or similar object.

13 Clean out any remaining fiber paper with water and a toothbrush. Clean the copper rings with fine steel wool.

14 Use the needle-nose pliers to attach the copper chain to the rings.

BASIC POCKET-VASE FUSE SCHEDULE

STAGE	FAHRENHEIT / CELSIUS
R1	400°F (222°C)/hour
L1	1420°F (771°C)
H1	15 minutes
R2	AFAP
L2	960°F (516°C)
H2	60 minutes

BLUE FLAME HANGING PANEL

An elegant addition to any room in your home, this panel offers subtle transitions between colors and a flowing, flame-like design. The template-cut flame shapes are surrounded by frit.

TOOLS AND MATERIALS

Midnight-blue transparent glass, 4 inches square (10.2 cm)

Cobalt-blue transparent glass, 6 x 7 inches (15.2 x 17.8 cm)

Light-blue transparent glass, 5 x 8 inches (12.7 x 20.3 cm)

Turquoise transparent glass, 8 inches square (20.3 cm)

Aqua transparent glass, 6 inches square (15.2 cm)

Clear glass, 11 x 13 inches (27.9 x 33 cm)

Fine transparent frit in turquoise, light blue, aqua, cobalt blue, and midnight blue

Basic Tools and Supplies (see page 16)

Glass grinder (optional)

Fuser's glue (optional)

Make-up spatula

Paintbrush

Diamond core drill bit, ⅜ inch (1 cm) in diameter (optional)

Drill press (optional)

Modeling clay (optional)

2 round hinged key rings, 1¼ inches (3.2 cm) in diameter, or S-hooks

Sturdy chain

INSTRUCTIONS

1 Use the Blue Flame Hanging Panel template (see page 124) as a pattern to cut out the midnight-blue, cobalt-blue, light-blue, turquoise, and aqua pieces. To remove any rough, uneven bits from the edges of the cut glass, use diamond hand pads or grind them with a glass grinder.

2 From the clear glass, measure and cut a 10 x 12-inch (25.4 x 30.5 cm) rectangle; two ½ x 12-inch (1.3 x 30.5 cm) strips; and two ½ x 9-inch (1.3 x 22.9 cm) strips. Wash and dry all the glass.

3 Position the 10 x 12-inch (25.4 x 30.5 cm) piece of clear glass over a copy of the Blue Flame Hanging Panel template. Arrange the colored pieces on the clear glass and place the four strips on top of its edges (photo 1). If you like, you can hold the pieces in place with fuser's glue.

4 Carefully transfer the glass to a prepared kiln shelf and fire it, using the Basic Tack-Fuse Schedule (see page 50). When the panel has cooled, remove it from the kiln.

5 Starting in the lower left-hand corner of the panel, use a spoon to fill the open areas between the design elements with fine frit. Place turquoise frit around the midnight blue glass pieces and shade it into light blue around the cobalt pieces. The light blue blends into the aqua, which flows around the top of the turquoise and up to the light blue pieces. Light blue gives way to cobalt, which in turn shades into midnight around the aqua pieces. Fill the open area at the bottom right with a blend of light blue and aqua frits. Mound the frit in the channels as high as you can without getting any on the panel design shapes. Use a dry paintbrush to keep the frit in the channels (photo 2) and to blend the colors in the large open area at the bottom right.

6 Place the panel on a prepared kiln shelf. Then fire it, using the Basic Fuse Schedule (see page 50).

7 To hang the panel, you'll need to drill two holes through it (see Drilling Holes on pages 57–58) or have someone do this for you. The holes should be made with a ⅜-inch (1 cm) diamond core drill bit and should be positioned 1 inch (2.5 cm) from the top of the panel and 1 inch (2.5 cm) in from each side.

8 Loop a key ring or S-hook through each hole and hang the panel with one or two lengths of sturdy chain.

SPRING GARDEN BIRDBATH

What red-breasted robin in its right mind could resist this stunning glass birdbath? The use of random-sized pieces of colored frit lends a special beauty to the design.

TOOLS AND MATERIALS

½ pound (227 g) each of transparent scrap glass in the following colors: cobalt blue, yellow, lime green, and turquoise

Clear iridescent glass, 18 inches square (45.7 cm)

½ pound (227 g) of clear medium frit

Basic Tools and Supplies (see page 16)

Kiln shelf at least 18 x 18 inches (45.7 x 45.7 cm)

Pillowcase and rubber band

Heavy-duty gardening gloves

Hammer

Shallow bowl mold, 16 inches (40.6 cm) in diameter

Wrought-iron birdbath stand to fit a 14- to 16-inch (35.6 x 40.6 cm) birdbath

INSTRUCTIONS

1 Wash and dry the scrap glass.

2 Place one of the colored glasses in a pillowcase and close the pillowcase with a rubber band. Put on your safety glasses and gloves. Hold the pillowcase securely, and smash it against a concrete floor several times. Take a look to see how large the crushed pieces are. Ideally, they should range from fine frit size to 1-inch-diameter (2.5 cm) chunks. If they're not small enough, close the pillowcase again and pound on it a few times with a hammer. (The ideal mix consists of mostly larger pieces, with some frit blended in for variety.) Pour the glass into a small dish and set it aside.

3 Repeat step 2 with each of the remaining colored glasses.

4 Cut a 16-inch-diameter (40.6 cm) circle from the clear iridescent glass. Wash and dry the circle.

5 Place the cut glass circle, iridescent side down, in the center of a prepared kiln shelf.

6 Sprinkle one-third of the clear frit evenly over the surface of the circle. This frit provides a base for the larger chunks of glass and helps minimize trapped air.

7 Sprinkle the colored glasses onto the circle, one at a time, arranging each one in a different area of the piece (photo 1). Yellow and lime green often react chemically with turquoise during firing, so you may see a dark line where they touch each other. You can determine the amount of reaction you get by your placement of the colors; the more they overlap, the more dark areas there will be in the finished piece.

8 Use the remaining clear frit to cover the entire surface of the base circle evenly, right up to its edges. If the edges of the circle aren't covered well, they'll pull in toward the center of the piece during firing and become uneven.

9 Fire the piece, using the Basic Fuse Schedule (page 50).

10 When the piece is cool, remove it from the kiln. Use diamond hand pads to smooth away any uneven, jagged bits around the edges. Any large popped air bubbles on the surface can be repaired with clear frit, and the piece can then be refired (see pages 60–61).

11 Wash and dry the piece. If your bowl mold is new, prepare it with kiln wash and let it dry completely.

12 Place the fused piece on the mold in the kiln.

13 Slump the piece, using the Basic Slump Schedule (see page 48). If it slumps unevenly, reposition the piece and slump it again.

BARGELLO PLATTER

The design of this platter is based on traditional bargello embroidery, which is characterized by fascinating zigzag swaths of color. Narrow strips of glass are arranged on their edges and then fused together.

INSTRUCTIONS

1 If your mold is new, prepare it with kiln wash and let it dry.

2 Use a strip-cutting system to cut all the glass into ⅜-inch-wide (1 cm) strips. Wash and dry all the strips.

3 Use a pencil to draw a 13 x 15-inch (33 x 38.1 cm) rectangle in the center of a prepared kiln shelf, pressing down hard enough to score the line into the kiln wash.

4 Place one of the dams along the 13-inch-long (33 cm) edge of the rectangle.

5 Bargello designs are filled with gentle curves and graceful swoops. The best way to lay out your piece is by starting with the color that will be in the center of the multicolored, zigzag pattern. Stand a strip of turquoise glass on edge against the side of the dam. (Note that every strip of glass in this project is placed on edge.)

6 Now press another turquoise strip tightly against the first one, positioning it so that its ends are either slightly higher or slightly lower than the ends of the

ESSENTIAL TIPS

- To create the ⅜-inch-wide (1 cm) glass strips for this platter, you'll cut across the width of each strip, not along its length. For example, the pieces you cut from the 48 inches (121.9 cm) of 4-inch-wide (10.2 cm) turquoise transparent glass will each be ⅜ inch (1 cm) wide and 4 inches (10.2 cm) long. When you've finished cutting all the glass in the Tools and Materials list, the shortest pieces will be 1 inch (2.5 cm) long and the longest will be 6 inches (15.2 cm).

- The dams won't be fired in the kiln, so they can consist of any rigid, flat material.

TOOLS AND MATERIALS

Turquoise transparent glass strips, 4 inches (10.2 cm) wide, total combined length of 48 inches (121.9 cm)

Cobalt-blue transparent glass strips, 2 inches (5.1 cm) wide, total combined length of 48 inches (121.9 cm)

Emerald-green transparent glass strips, 3 inches (7.6 cm) wide, total combined length of 48 inches (121.9 cm)

Clear glass strips in the following dimensions:
1 x 18 inches (2.5 x 45.7 cm)
2 inches (5.1 cm) wide, total combined length of 22 inches (55.9 cm)
3 inches (7.6 cm) wide, total combined length of 25 inches (63.5 cm)
4 x 12 inches (10.2 x 30.5 cm)
5 inches (12.7 cm) wide, total combined length of 20 inches (50.8 cm)
6 x 7 inches (15.2 x 17.8 cm)

Basic Tools and Supplies (see page 16)

Strip-cutting system

Kiln shelf, at least 15 x 17 inches (38.1 x 43.2 cm)

2 dams, each ½ x 1 x 13 inches (1.3 x 2.5 x 33 cm)

Soft paintbrush

Tile saw (optional)

Glass grinder (optional)

Rectangular slump mold, 13 x 15 inches (33 x 38.1 cm)

first strip. The farther apart the ends of the two strips are, the steeper the curve in your design will be. The closer together they are, the gentler the curve will be. Never position two adjacent pieces so their ends are even. To create a flowing design, position several strips so that each one is slightly higher than the one before it; then change directions with the next several strips so that each one is slightly lower than the last. If the cut edge of a strip is so uneven that the strip leans and falls over instead of standing up, either turn it around so the direction of the lean is towards the strips already in place, or turn it upside down so that you're working with the opposite edge, which may be smoother.

7 When you've positioned enough turquoise strips to stretch one-third of the way across the rectangle, it's time to fill in the areas above and below the turquoise strips with the other colors and clear glass (photo 1). Some people like to complete one color at a time, all the way across the rectangle. I prefer to lay out about one-third of the center color, then go back and fill in these columns with other colors, so I can watch the full design as it develops and monitor how many of the different-sized clear strips I've used. To complete each column, first place a strip of cobalt blue glass against the dam, with its bottom end touching the top end of the turquoise piece below it. Then position a strip of emerald green glass under the turquoise. Once you've completed these columns with these colors, finish them

off with clear glass. Because the clear glass strips are of different lengths, these pieces will overlap the top and bottom edges of the rectangle by ¼ to 1¼ inch (6.4 mm to 2.5 cm). Choose a clear strip to place below the green that won't extend by more than 1 inch (2.5 cm) over the bottom line. Place another clear strip on top of the cobalt so it extends over the top line by no more than 1 inch (2.5 cm). In some columns, you may want to place only one clear strip so that your colored pattern runs all the way to the top or bottom of the rectangle.

8 Finish filling in with clear pieces until you're one-third of the way across the rectangle. Each column should contain a turquoise, green, blue, and one or two clear strips. Keep track of how many clear pieces you're using in each size. If you run short, you can always shift your design up or down to use clear strips of different lengths. When you've finished all the columns, use the remaining dam to press the glass in from the right-hand edge.

9 Before firing, use a toothpick or similar object to push each column of glass up or down from the top or bottom until the pieces fit snugly together. Make sure all the top and bottom pieces still extend over the top and bottom edges of the rectangle. Use the soft paintbrush to remove any dust.

10 Place the kiln shelf in the kiln and remove the two dams. Fire the strips, using the Basic Fuse Schedule (see page 50).

11 The side edges of the fired piece should be fairly smooth, but the top and bottom edges will be uneven, so you'll need to cut them. You'll see faint ridges on the underside of the fired piece, along the top and bottom edges; these were created by the scored pencil lines you made on the kiln shelf. Using these two ridges as guides, mark lines across the top and bottom of the upper surface of the glass. (If you don't see a ridge, you can measure the piece to decide where to mark these lines. They should be 13 inches (33 cm) apart, perpendicular to the sides, and at least ¼ inch (6.4 mm) in from the top and bottom edges.)

12 If you're comfortable cutting very thick pieces by hand, use your cutter and a straightedge to cut along the marked lines. A tile saw will make this job much easier.

13 Use diamond hand pads or a glass grinder to smooth the edges and round them slightly. Finish the grinding with a 220-grit diamond hand pad so the edges will shine back up in the slump. An alternative to grinding is to place the piece on a prepared kiln shelf and fire it, using the Basic Fire-Polish Schedule (see page 51).

14 Wash and dry the piece. Place the piece on the mold in the kiln.

15 Fire the piece, using the Basic Slump Schedule (see page 48).

CHECKERBOARD AND CHECKERS

This charming set is a little smaller than the tournament variety, but its colors are much more attractive. The squares on the board are backed by an opal glass base.

TOOLS AND MATERIALS

*6 pieces of olive-green transparent glass,
each 1¹⁵⁄₃₂ x 19 inches (3.7 x 48.3 cm)*

*6 pieces of French-vanilla opal glass,
each 1¹⁵⁄₃₂ x 19 inches (3.7 x 48.3 cm)*

*French-vanilla opal glass, 12 inches square
(30.5 cm)*

Basic Tools and Supplies (see page 16)

Small circle cutter

Glass grinder (optional)

ESSENTIAL TIPS

- When I try to put together as many square pieces as this checkerboard requires, the assembled piece always seems to grow a little bit. To get all 64 pieces to fit on the base, I cut each one ¹⁄₃₂ inch (.8 mm) under the required 1½ inch-square (3.8 cm) size. I also like to cut long strips from the glass first and then cut the squares from them.

- A small circle cutter is invaluable for cutting the checker pieces. Cutting them is also a good time to practice flipping the glass over after you've made the score and running the score from the back (see page 41).

- When I have to cut this many circles, I start with strips of glass ½ inch (1.3 cm) wider than the circle diameters and cut the circles in a row from each strip. This makes it easy to keep track of my scores and minimizes glass wastage, too.

INSTRUCTIONS

1 To make the checkerboard pieces, cut 32 olive-green transparent glass squares and 32 French-vanilla opal glass squares from the strips; each of these 64 pieces should be 1¹⁵⁄₃₂ inches square (3.7 cm). You'll use the remaining olive-green and French-vanilla glass to make the checkers.

2 Wash and dry all the glass squares.

3 Arrange the small squares on a prepared kiln shelf in eight rows, with eight squares in each row. Remember to alternate the colors (photo 1). Square up all the corners when you're finished.

4 Center the 12-inch (30.5 cm) French-vanilla opal square on top of the small squares and fire the assembled board, using the Basic Fuse Schedule (see page 50). This checkerboard is fused upside down so that its surface lines will remain crisp and straight.

5 When the checkerboard is cool, remove it from the kiln.

BASIC SMALL-OBJECT LOW-FUSE SCHEDULE

STAGE	FAHRENHEIT / CELSIUS
R1	600°F (333°C)/hour
L1	1425°F (774°C)
H1	10 minutes
R2	AFAP
L2	960°F (516°C)
H2	30 minutes

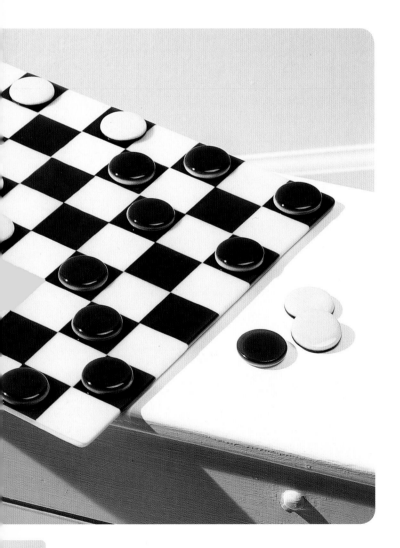

6 Cut 26 circles, each 1¼ inches (3.2 cm) in diameter, from the remaining olive-green glass, and 26 from the French-vanilla glass. You only need 12 checkers for each player (each checker is made up of two circles), but cutting 52 circles will give you one extra checker for each player in case any are lost or broken.

7 Using diamond hand pads or a glass grinder, grind away any rough edges from the circles, then wash and dry them.

8 Place 13 circles of each color on a prepared kiln shelf, spacing them at least ¼ inch (6.4 mm) apart. Stack a circle of the opposite color on top of each one. You want to do more than tack fuse the checkers, but you don't want to fully fuse them, or they'll lose their crisp shapes. Fire them, using the Basic Small-Object Low-Fuse Schedule on this page.

9 When the checkers are cool, remove them from the kiln.

10 (This step and step 11 are optional; if your board surface is already perfect, just skip them.) Sometimes when you fuse a piece face down on the kiln shelf, hazing and other imperfections can appear on the surface. Use diamond hand pads to remove or smooth out any imperfections on your checkerboard, then wash and dry it.

11 To remove any remaining scratches or roughness from the checkerboard surface and give it a glossy shine, place the board on a prepared kiln shelf, squares-side up, and fire it, using the Basic Fire-Polish Schedule (see page 51).

This opaque sculptural piece doesn't require transmitted light to show off the beauty of its brilliant colors. The secret to achieving its distinctive glass pattern is to melt the glass in an orchid pot instead of in a regular terra-cotta flowerpot.

TOOLS AND MATERIALS

1 pound (454 g) each of 90 COE scrap glass in the following colors: yellow opal, orange opal, lime-green opal, yellow transparent, orange transparent, and lime-green transparent

3 to 4 ounces (85 to 113.4 g) of 90 COE lime-green transparent medium frit

¼ ounce (7.1 g) of 90 COE lime-green transparent large frit

Basic Tools and Supplies (see page 16)

Small, motorized grinding tool, with grinding bit for ceramic that will fit through the holes in the orchid pot

Terra-cotta orchid pot, 6 inches (15.2 cm) in diameter at its top

4 pieces of mullite, each ½ x 1 x 1 inch (1.3 x 2.5 x 2.5 cm)

Pillowcase (optional)

Wheeled nippers

2 mullite dams, each 1 inch (2.5 cm) wide and at least 6 inches (15.2 cm) long

2 mullite dams, each ¾ x 1 x 20 inches (1.9 x 2.5 x 50.8 cm)

Shelf paper, 18 x 18 inches (45.7 x 45.7 cm)

Glass grinder

Paintbrush

Display stand for 16-inch-diameter (40.6 cm) fused glass panel

Vinyl pads (optional)

INSTRUCTIONS

1 Prepare the kiln shelf (see Essential Tips) with 12 to 20 coats of kiln wash and let it dry completely.

2 Use the small, motorized grinding tool and ceramic bit to enlarge the slits in the orchid pot and extend them to the bottom of the pot (photo 1).

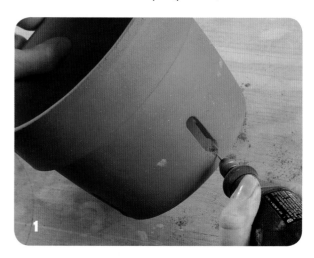

3 Wipe the entire pot with a damp cloth to remove any terra-cotta dust.

4 Place the four pieces of mullite on the kiln floor to serve as ½-inch-tall (1.3 cm) posts for the kiln shelf. Set the kiln shelf on top of them.

5 Cut the glass into strips no longer than 6 inches (15.2 cm) each. Stand the strips upright in the orchid pot. Don't use kiln wash or any other release agent on the pot; it will flake off and contaminate your melt.

6 Place the two shorter mullite dams on the left and right edges of the kiln shelf so they're 1 inch (2.5 cm) in height (photo 2). Place the two long mullite dams on top of and perpendicular to them, positioning these upper dams to be 1 inch (2.5 cm) in height, as well. Place them 2 to 3 inches (5.1 to 7.6 cm) apart and center them over the shelf.

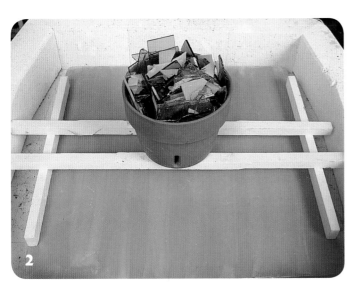

2

- An orchid pot differs from a regular flowerpot in that it has four drainage slits around the sides, as well as a drainage hole in the bottom.

- This project requires a kiln with a clearance of at least 12 inches (30.5 cm) between the floor and the top elements, and a kiln shelf at least 18 x 18 inches (45.7 x 45.7 cm).

- In this project, the glass is prepared by cutting it into strips. If you prefer, you can crush the glass in a pillowcase instead (see the Spring Garden Birdbath instructions on page 93) or break the glass into pieces with wheeled nippers. Then pour the glass into the orchid pot. (If it won't all fit, crush it some more.)

7 Place the filled pot on the second set of strips, above the center of the kiln shelf. As the glass melts, it will flow from all the holes in the pot, so make sure the holes are completely clear of the strips.

8 If your kiln lid opens upward, measure the distance from the top edge of the glass in the pot to the bottom inner surface of the kiln lid to make sure no glass will touch the lid or elements when the lid is closed.

9 Fire the piece, using the Basic Melt-Fuse Schedule on page 104.

10 When the kiln is cool, remove the orchid pot and dams. You're likely to find stringers of glass connecting the pot to the glass underneath. Use wheeled nippers to cut these close to the surface of the piece.

11 Remove your piece from the kiln. You'll probably need to remove kiln wash that has stuck to its back (see page 55).

12 Place an 18 x 18-inch (45.7 x 45.7 cm) piece of shelf paper on the kiln shelf and use a pencil to draw a 16-inch-diameter (40.6 cm) circle on it. Center your finished piece inside the circle. Using a black permanent marker, mark any areas on the glass that extend beyond the circle, then remove the excess glass with the glass grinder. Don't worry about any areas of the piece that don't reach all the way out to the drawn circle. If you'd like a frit border all the way around your piece, make sure there's at least ¼ inch (6.4 mm) between the edge of the piece and the drawn circle.

13 Clean and dry your piece, and place it back inside the circle on the shelf paper.

14 Inspect the top surface for popped air bubbles. Ignore the tiny ones—melts almost always have some. To repair larger, more noticeable bubbles (whether popped or not), use an awl and some large frit (see pages 60–61).

15 As shown in photo 3, fill in the spaces between the edges of the piece and the drawn circle with the medium frit, to a depth of ³⁄₁₆ inch (4.8 mm).

16 Fire the piece, using the Basic Fuse Schedule (see page 50).

17 When the kiln has cooled completely, remove the piece, clean it, and put it in the display stand. If it's a bit too large, grind and fire polish it, using the Basic Fire-Polish Schedule (see page 51). If it's too small, fit vinyl pads (often used to protect tables and floors) into the display frame to hold the piece more securely.

BASIC MELT-FUSE SCHEDULE

STAGE	FAHRENHEIT / CELSIUS
R1	600°F (333°C)/hour
L1	1650°F (899°C)
H1	90 minutes
R2	AFAP
L2	960°F (516°C)
H2	60 minutes
R3	180°F (100°C)/hour
L3	700°F (371°C)
H3	Off

CRANBERRY "STONE" PLATTER

No matter what you serve on this platter, your guests will probably eat every bite just to reveal the fascinating design. To create it, glass is placed on wire mesh, then melted into a lined, oval-shaped cut-out area in layered fiber paper beneath the screen.

TOOLS AND MATERIALS

1½ pounds (680 g) of clear glass

¾ pound (340 g) of 90 COE coral tint glass

¼ pound (113 g) of 90 COE French-vanilla opal glass

½ pound (227 g) of 90 COE apricot opal glass

¼ pound (113 g) of 90 COE coral transparent glass

Clear 90 COE large frit (optional)

Basic Tools and Supplies (see page 16)

2 pieces of fiber paper, each ⅛ x 15 x 27 inches (3.2 mm x 38.1 cm x 68.6 cm)

Strips of fiber paper, each ⅛ inch (3.2 mm) thick x 1 inch (2.5 cm) wide, total combined length of 45 inches (114.3 cm)

Welded stainless mesh, 24 inches square (61 cm), ½-inch (1.3 cm) mesh size, .047-inch-diameter (1.2 mm) wire

2 mullite dams, each ½ x 2½ x 20 inches (1.3 x 6.4 x 50.8 cm)

2 mullite dams, each ½ x 1 x 15 inches (1.3 x 2.5 x 38.1 cm)

Heavy-duty gardening gloves

Heavy-duty wire cutters or tin snips

8 kiln posts, each 4 inches (10.2 cm) in height

Oval platter mold, 7 x 19 inches (17.8 x 48.3 cm)

Glass grinder (optional)

Overspray (optional)

Airbrush sprayer (optional)

INSTRUCTIONS

1 Prepare a kiln shelf with 20 to 25 coats of kiln wash.

2 Stack the two rectangles of fiber paper, smooth sides up, on your work surface. Center the oval platter mold upside down on top of them and trace around it with a pencil. Draw another line, ⅛ inch (3.2 mm) out from your traced line. Use a craft knife to cut through both pieces of fiber paper along the outermost line.

3 Place the stacked rectangles on the dry kiln shelf, with the oval running diagonally. Use the craft knife to trim the fiber-paper edges that extend out over the shelf, and cut out triangles at the corners to make room for the kiln posts.

4 Line the inside of the oval cutout with the strips of fiber paper (photo 1). Pack them in tightly and cut the last one so it fits snugly against the edge of the first one. The longer the strips, the more even the edge of your fused oval will be, but cutting a single strip isn't essential; two or three will work fine. Set the kiln shelf aside.

5 Refer to photo 2 to help you with the next several steps. To construct the mesh frame, first place the welded stainless mesh flat on your work surface. Arrange the four mullite dams on top of it to create a 20-inch-square (50.8 cm) frame in the center.

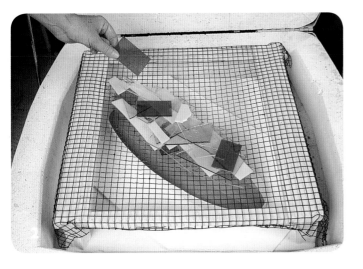

diamond hand pads or a glass grinder to smooth and even any rough edges of the melt. If the melt has any bubbles, use the instructions on pages 60–61 to repair them. If your piece has none, skip to step 13.

11 Wash and dry the oval. If you want to use an overspray, apply it now.

12 Place the melt on a prepared shelf, and fire it, using the Basic Fuse Schedule (see page 50).

13 If your mold is new, prepare it with kiln wash and let it dry completely.

14 Slump the oval into the mold, using the Basic Slump Schedule (see page 48).

6 Put on the heavy-duty gardening gloves. Using the wire cutters or tin snips, cut two 2-inch-long (5.1 cm) slits on each edge of the mesh, each 3 inches (7.6 cm) in from a corner. (You'll cut a total of eight slits, two at each corner.) Now use pliers to wrap the long edge of the mesh between each pair of slits up and around a mullite dam. Fold the corners down so they'll lie along the sides of the kiln posts that will rest underneath the frame.

7 Place four of the kiln posts on the kiln floor, on their sides. Set the kiln shelf, with the lined, fiber-paper cutout on it, on top of them. Stand the remaining four kiln posts upright on the shelf, one at each corner. Flip the screen and mullite frame over so the wrapped edges are on the bottom, and place the frame on the kiln posts.

8 Cut the glass for the melt into pieces that are small enough for you to arrange on the mesh, but not so small that they'll fall through the mesh holes. Wash and dry the glass. Arrange the glass on the screen, distributing it evenly, directly over the oval cutout.

9 Fire the glass, using the Basic Melt-Fuse Schedule (see page 104).

10 When the fused glass oval from the melt has cooled, remove it from the kiln and use diamond hand pads to remove any kiln wash that has stuck to the back. Use

LACE WALL SCONCE

Why settle for a generic wall sconce? Make your own stunning, one-of-a-kind glass sconce shade. Once you've learned how to make the fiber-blanket mold for this shade, you can create an entire series of distinctive sconces.

TOOLS AND MATERIALS

White opal glass, 12 inches square (30.5 cm)

½ pound (227 g) of transparent cobalt-blue medium frit

Basic Tools and Supplies (see page 16)

Fiber blanket, ½ x 12 x 12 inches (1.3 x 30.5 x 30.5 cm)

Commercial wall sconce with hardware and glass shade

Plastic tray, at least 1 x 13 x 13 inches (2.5 x 33 x 33 cm)

Fiber-blanket hardener

Long, flat-bladed knife or similar tool

Drywall sanding paper

Paper for template

Kiln shelf, at least 12 inches (30.5 cm) in diameter

Shelf paper to fit the kiln shelf

Cloth measuring tape

Small paintbrush

Overspray (optional)

Airbrush sprayer (optional)

Small hair (or craft) dryer (optional)

2 kiln posts, each 3 inches (7.6 cm) tall

ESSENTIAL TIP

You'll make your own mold for this project by shaping a piece of fiber blanket to the inner surface of a commercial glass sconce shade like the ones found at home-improvement stores. Find a sconce you like and adjust the sizes of the fiber blanket and glass accordingly.

INSTRUCTIONS

1 Spread the fiber blanket on your work surface and roll the commercial shade across it from edge to edge, pressing down firmly (photo 1). Use scissors to cut the blanket around the impression left by the sconce, ½ inch (1.3 cm) out from that outline's edge.

2 Place the fiber-blanket cutout in the plastic tray. Put on your rubber dishwashing gloves and cover the blanket with fiber-blanket hardener, wetting the blanket thoroughly.

3 Because hardener sticks to glass as it dries, you'll need to apply a release to the commercial shade before you shape the fiber blanket in it. Gently mix 1 tablespoon (14.8 ml) of dishwashing detergent with 1 tablespoon (14.8 ml) of water. Smear this solution thickly onto the entire inner surface of the glass shade.

4 Press the wet fiber blanket down into the solution-coated shade. Your goals are to squeeze out all the air bubbles, create a smooth fiber-blanket surface where the blanket contacts the glass, and define a ridge in the blanket that will indicate the exterior edges of the finished shade size. Your original blanket measurements were based on the exterior outline of the glass shade, but because the blanket is now pressed into the smaller interior of the shade, it extends by more than the ½ inch

(1.3 cm) that you added when you cut it out. Trim the blanket edges back to leave an even ½ inch (1.3 cm) extending from the edges of the shade.

5 A hardening fiber blanket can take several days to dry out at room temperature. To reduce this time considerably, you can kiln-dry the blanket instead. Place the fiber blanket (still in the glass shade) in the kiln, with the blanket facing up and the shade supported by kiln posts so it won't roll over. Heat them slowly—about 50°F (27.8°C) per hour—keeping the kiln temperature at or below 175°F (79°C), for several hours. Cool the mold, and if it isn't dry to the touch, repeat. You may vent the kiln during this process, but don't open it. Acrid fumes will be released during venting, so make sure your work area is well ventilated. Never harden a mold in your oven; the fumes can contaminate your food.

6 When the mold is completely dry and hard, gently remove it from the shade, using a flat-bladed knife or similar tool to pry it loose if necessary. If the mold has soft spots or is too soft to support the weight of the glass during firing, you may not have applied enough hardener; you'll need to make a new mold.

7 Prefire the new mold to 1300°F (704°C), then turn the kiln off.

8 The surface of the mold is likely to be a little rough. You can smooth it with drywall sanding paper (be sure to wear your particulate respirator), but I prefer to fill in the rough surface with a kiln-wash paste made by slowly mixing water into ¼ cup (59.1 ml) of dry kiln wash until the paste is the consistency of mayonnaise. Before applying the paste, use a haik brush to apply some regular kiln-wash solution to the exterior of the mold (photo 2). Then, using your fingers, smooth the paste over the mold to fill in any imperfections. Allow the paste to dry.

9 The thick paste will crack as it dries. To remove any small cracks, put on your particulate respirator and use drywall sanding paper to lightly sand only the surface of the kiln wash—not the mold—until it's smooth. Don't remove any of the dust. Moisten your fingers with water and smooth them over the mold to turn the dust into

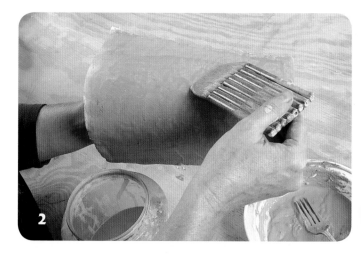

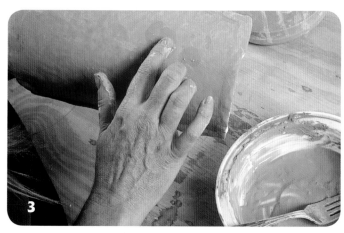

a light paste again (photo 3). Blend in all the dust and evenly moisten the surface without making it too wet. Set the mold aside to dry.

10 To make a template for cutting your glass, either roll the commercial shade across a sheet of paper, tracing it with a pencil as you go, or use a ruler and pencil to draw the shape. Use the paper template to mark and cut the white opal glass.

11 Place the shelf paper on the kiln shelf.

12 Place the glass that you cut out in step 10 in the middle of the shelf paper and trace around it with a pencil. Set the glass aside.

13 Pour the cobalt-blue frit into the middle of the traced pattern. With a dry paintbrush, create swirls and thick lines of frit that extend to the edges of the pattern (photo 4).

14 Fuse the lace, using the Basic Fuse Schedule (see page 50).

15 When the lace has cooled, remove it from the kiln. Use diamond hand pads or a small, motorized grinding tool to smooth away any uneven or jagged areas on the edges. Wash and dry the lace, and set it aside.

16 Wash and dry the white opal base and place it on a prepared kiln shelf. Set the lace on top of the base, shiny side up, making sure that it doesn't overlap the edges. Although an overspray isn't absolutely necessary, you're likely to achieve a better surface and a better flow between the lace and the base glass if you apply an overspray before fusing them. Use the airbrush sprayer to cover the surface with a light, even coat of overspray (photo 5). Due to the different heights and overlapping of the two layers of glass, I like to apply a few coats to make sure I get complete coverage. You can speed up the drying of the overspray by using a small hair (or craft) dryer.

17 Place the shelf in the kiln and fire the piece, using the Basic Low-Fuse Schedule on this page.

18 Using the cloth measuring tape and a permanent black marker, find and mark the center of the top and bottom edges of the impression left by the sconce in the fiber-blanket mold. Set the mold in the kiln, with the smaller end sitting on the two kiln posts so that the upper surface of the mold is level.

19 Wash and dry the fused sconce panel. Find and mark the center of its top and bottom edges. Then place it, lace side up, on the mold, using the marks on the panel and mold to align the panel correctly. Fire the piece, using the Basic Slump Schedule (see page 48).

BASIC LOW-FUSE SCHEDULE

STAGE	FAHRENHEIT / CELSIUS
R1	400°F (222°C)/hour
L1	1425°F (774°C)
H1	10 minutes
R2	AFAP
L2	960°F (516°C)
H2	60 minutes
R3	150°F (83°C)/hour
L3	700°F (371°C)
H3	Off

PATTERN-BAR MIRROR FRAME

You may not see much of yourself in this mirror, only because you won't be able to tear your eyes from the frame. The design is created by fusing two blocks of glass strips, all placed on edge, then cutting the blocks into smaller sections and fusing those sections together.

INSTRUCTIONS

1 Wash and dry the strips of glass.

2 Place the largest piece of fiber paper in the middle of the kiln shelf so its 20-inch-long (50.8 cm) edges are at the left and right. Stand one of the 16-inch-long (40.6 cm) dams along the left edge of the paper. Line the interior surface of the dam with one of the 16-inch-long (40.6 cm) fiber-paper strips (see Essential Tips).

3 Using figure 1 and photo 1 as guides, stand a ¼-inch-wide (6.4 mm) black strip on edge against the fiber paper. Continue by positioning the next 11 strips in the pattern, pressing them tightly together. Place another 16-inch-long (40.6 cm) strip of fiber paper against the last strip of glass and add another 16-inch-long (40.6 cm) dam.

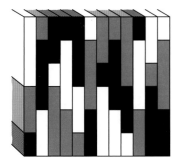

Figure 1

TOOLS AND MATERIALS

Glass strips, each 16 inches (40.6 cm) long, in the following colors and widths:

Red opal
    4 strips, ¼ inch (6.4 mm)
    16 strips, ½ inch (1.3 cm)
    4 strips, ¾ inch (1.9 cm)
French vanilla
    4 strips, ¼ inch (6.4 mm)
    4 strips, ½ inch (1.3 mm)
    16 strips, ¾ inch (1.9 cm)
Black
    16 strips, ¼ inch (6.4 mm)
    4 strips, ½ inch (1.3 cm)
    4 strips, ¾ inch (1.9 cm)

Basic Tools and Supplies (see page 16)

Fiber paper, ⅛-inch (3.2 mm) thick, in the following dimensions:

    1 piece, 10 x 20 inches (25.4 x 50.8 cm)
    4 pieces, each 2 x 16 inches (5.1 x 40.6 cm)
    2 pieces, each 2 x 8 inches (5.1 x 20.3 cm)

Mullite dams, ¾-inch (1.9 cm) thick, in the following dimensions:

    3 dams, each 2 x 16 inches (5.1 x 40.6 cm)
    2 dams, each 2 x 8 inches (5.1 x 20.3 cm)

Four kiln posts

Fiber blanket, 1 x 20 x 20 inches (2.5 x 50.8 x 50.8 cm)

Glass grinder (optional)

Tile saw

Overspray

Airbrush sprayer

Small hair (or craft) dryer (optional)

Mirror, ⅛ x 9 x 12 inches (3.2 mm x 22.9 cm x 30.5 cm)

Double-sided foam mounting tape, 4-foot-long (121.9 cm) roll, ½-inch (1.3 cm) wide

Adhesive (see Essential Tips on page 114)

Picture-hanging hardware, with metal loops

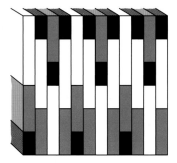

Figure 2

- Although pattern bars are easier to construct by stacking the glass strips flat on the shelf, I like to build mine with the strips on edge so that when the glass melts, gravity pulls it down through the vertical lines instead of across them.

- To give the smoothest surface to the pattern bars, always position the fiber paper that lines the dams around the bars so that the smooth side of the paper faces the glass.

- The shorter dams don't have to be exactly 8 inches (20.3 cm) long; they can be between that length and the width of the shelf under them.

- To keep crisp, sharp lines in a geometric piece, fuse it face down on the kiln shelf and then flip it over and fire polish it. For this project, we do a low fuse instead of a fire polish because the overspray must be fired to at least 1400°F (760°C).

- One of the best adhesives for attaching glass to metal is available in the rearview-mirror adhesive kits sold at automotive stores.

4 Fill in the upper rows of the pattern bar.

5 Position another long piece of fiber paper against the outer surface of the second dam. Then, using the layout in figure 2, construct the second pattern bar next to the first one. Finish by adding the fourth long piece of fiber paper and the third long dam.

6 Position an 8-inch-long (20.3 cm) piece of fiber paper against each short end of the pattern bars. Press the remaining two dams against these pieces of fiber paper (see Essential Tips). Prop each dam up with a kiln post.

7 Fire the piece, using the Basic Pattern-Bar Fuse Schedule on the next page. As the firing approaches the anneal cycle—somewhere around 1000°F (537.8°C)— turn off the kiln, open it (follow the safety precautions on pages 34–35), and place the fiber-blanket square across the top of the pattern bars to help them cool more evenly. Close the lid and turn the kiln back on. The only disadvantage to this step is getting your kiln controller back to the correct segment of the firing (the anneal stage) when you turn it back on. With one of my kilns, I have to create and use a new firing schedule that has only the anneal and cool-down segments of the original firing in it. Read your controller's manual or call the manufacturer if you need help.

8 When the pattern bars are completely cool, remove them from the kiln and wash them.

9 Use diamond hand pads or a glass grinder to remove any rough edges from the corners.

10 Using the tile saw, cut the bars into ⅜-inch-thick (1 cm) slices (photo 2). Then wash and dry them.

11 To create the frame, lay out the pattern-bar slices on a prepared kiln shelf in any order and orientation you like. The frame is eight squares across and ten squares down, and each side is two squares wide. Line up the squares evenly and tightly. The front of the mirror frame is face down on the kiln shelf during this firing.

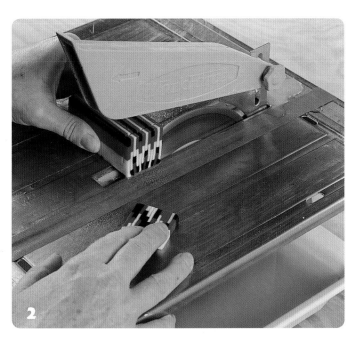

2

12 Fuse the frame, using the Basic Fuse Schedule (see page 50).

13 Use diamond hand pads to remove any kiln wash or hazing from the surface of the frame that rested on the kiln shelf during the last firing. The next firing will remove scratches, but it won't remove surface contamination.

14 Place the frame on the kiln shelf, with the surface that was face down during the first firing now facing up. Using an airbrush sprayer, apply overspray evenly to the frame's top surface and edges. Dry it with the small hair (or craft) dryer or let it air-dry; then apply another coat. Fire the frame, using the Basic Low-Fuse Schedule on page 111.

15 To attach the mirror to the frame, I use double-sided foam mounting tape; it holds well and blocks any light that might otherwise appear between the frame and mirror. Peel the paper from one surface of the tape and adhere the tape to the front of the mirror, all along its edges. Remove the paper backing from the tape. Center your frame, face up, over the mirror and press it down gently onto the tape.

16 Set the framed mirror face down on your work surface. Using your small, motorized grinding tool, roughen the glass areas where you'd like to attach the metal picture-hanging loops; also roughen the backs of the metal loops. Attach the loops to the frame, following the directions that came with the adhesive.

17 Either hook the metal loops onto two picture hangers attached to the wall, or attach a wire to the loops and hook the wire over a single hanger. If you choose the latter method, follow the directions on the wire package to attach the wire to the loops.

BASIC PATTERN-BAR FUSE SCHEDULE

STAGE	FAHRENHEIT / CELSIUS
R1	600°F (333°C)/hour
L1	1150°F (621°C)
H1	0 minutes
R2	180°F (100°C)/hour
L2	1250°F (677°C)
H2	10 minutes
R3	AFAP
L3	1500°F (816°C)
H3	30 minutes
R4	AFAP
L4	960°F (516°C)
H4	180 minutes
R5	16°F (9°C)/hour
L5	750°F (399°C)
H5	0 minutes
R6	32°F (18°C)/hour
L6	650°F (343°C)
H6	Off

SPLIT-LEAF PHILODENDRON FOUNTAIN

Soothe your troubles away and treat yourself to a visual delight with this beautiful fountain in aqua and blue. Its elegant layered shape, molded glass leaves, and gently trickling water are perfectly designed to induce a meditative, peaceful state of mind.

INSTRUCTIONS

Making the Three Fountain Layers

1 Cut one 16-inch-diameter (40.6 cm) circle from the steel-blue glass and another from the clear glass. Cut two 13-inch-diameter (33 cm) circles from the two 15-inch (38.1 cm) aqua glass squares. Cut two 11-inch-diameter (27.8 cm) circles from the 13-inch (33 cm) light-blue and aqua glass squares. Wash and dry the glass circles.

2 Stack the two 15-inch (38.1 cm) fiber-paper squares on your work surface, rough side up. Center one of the 13-inch (33 cm) glass circles on top of them and trace around the glass with a pencil. Then draw another circle around the first circle, 14 inches (35.6 cm) in diameter. This outer circle, which will serve as a cutting line, doesn't need to be perfect; it only needs to be larger than the glass.

3 Repeat step 2 with the 13-inch (33 cm) fiber-paper squares and one 11-inch (27.8 cm) glass circle, drawing an exterior circle roughly 12 inches (30.5 cm) in diameter.

ESSENTIAL TIP

To make the three glass layers for this fountain, first you'll create three fiber-paper molds, one for each layer. Two of these molds will each consist of two layered circles of fiber paper; the bottom circle will be solid, and the top circle will have leaf-shaped cut-out areas in it, as well as fiber-paper leaf shapes placed on top of it. The mold for the bottom layer (the fountain bowl) will consist of a single circle of fiber paper, with leaf-shaped cutouts placed on top of it.

TOOLS AND MATERIALS

Steel-blue transparent glass, 17 inches square (43.2 cm)

Clear glass, 17 inches square (43.2 cm)

2 pieces of aqua transparent glass, each 15 inches square (38.1 cm)

Light-blue transparent glass, 13 inches square (33 cm)

Aqua transparent glass, 13 inches square (33 cm)

Clear glass, 4½ x 16 inches (11.4 x 40.6 cm)

¼ pound (113 g) of fine frit, aqua transparent

¼ pound (113 g) of fine frit, light-blue transparent

Fiber paper, ⅛-inch (3.2 mm) thick, in the following dimensions:

2 pieces, each 15 inches square (38.1 cm)
2 pieces, each 13 inches square (33 cm)
2 pieces, each 18 inches square (45.7 cm)
1 strip, 3 x 18 inches (7.6 x 45.7 cm)
2 strips, each 1 x 16 inches (2.5 x 40.6 cm)
2 strips, each 1 x 3 inches (2.5 x 7.6 cm)
12 pieces, each 3 inches square (7.6 cm)

Basic Tools and Supplies (see page 16)

Bowl mold, 3 inches (7.6 cm) deep and 16 inches (40.6 cm) in diameter

2 mullite dams, each 1 x 16 inches (2.5 x 40.6 cm)

2 mullite dams, each 1 x 3 inches (2.5 x 7.6 cm)

Diamond core drill bit, ⅝ inch (1.6 cm) in diameter (optional)

Drill press (optional)

Modeling clay (optional)

Tile saw

Clear tubing, 3½ inches (8.9 cm) long, ½-inch (1.3 cm) outer diameter

Submersible fountain pump 80 GPH (.0842 L/sec)

Small submersible fountain light (optional)

4 Repeat step 2 with one (not both) of the 18-inch (45.7 cm) fiber-paper squares and a 16-inch (40.6 cm) glass circle, drawing an exterior circle roughly 17 inches (43.2 cm) in diameter. Set the other 18-inch (45.7 cm) fiber-paper square aside.

5 Using a craft knife, cut out the fiber-paper circles along the outer penciled lines. You'll end up with a total of five circles. (Unless you're instructed otherwise, make sure that all the fiber paper you use in the rest of this project is placed rough side up.)

6 Trace one Medium Leaf template and one Small Leaf template (see page 125) onto one of the 12-inch (30.5 cm) fiber-paper circles, positioning them to leave enough room for a medium-sized leaf and arranging the traced shapes so they—and the space you've left for the medium-sized leaf—are equidistant. (Positioning a leaf template so it overlaps the edge of the penciled circle slightly can provide an interesting effect in the fused piece.) Cut out the two leaves with the craft knife. (If you overlapped the edge of the penciled circle with a leaf template, don't cut all the way out to the edge of the paper circle. Just cut to and along the edge of the penciled circle.) Set the small leaf pieces aside. Position the medium leaf pieces in the space that you left for them on the circle. Place the circle, with the medium leaf assembled on it, and the small and medium leaf cutout areas in it, on top of the other 12-inch (30.5 cm) circle. Set the stacked circles aside.

7 Use photo 1 as a guide for this step. Place the small leaf pieces from step 6 on one of the 14-inch (45.6 cm) fiber-paper circles, anywhere toward the edge of the penciled inner circle. Trace the Large Leaf template (see page 125) onto this circle, positioning it to leave enough room for another large leaf. Cut out the large leaf you just traced. Set aside the teardrop shape from this leaf.

Move the other two pieces of the large leaf to the space you left on this circle for a large leaf. Place the circle, with the small and large leaves assembled on it, on top of the other 14-inch (30.5 cm) circle. Place the teardrop shape back in the large leaf cut-out area and set the stack aside.

8 Using the Small, Medium, and Large Leaf templates, draw as many leaves of all three sizes as will fit comfortably on the 18-inch (45.7 cm) square of fiber paper. Be creative; cut any combination of sizes that appeals to you. Cut out these leaves and set them aside.

9 Place the 17-inch (43.2 cm) fiber-paper circle in front of you and arrange the leaf shapes from step 8 on top of it. Turn the shapes in different directions, arranging them for a balanced, uncrowded effect.

10 Now it's time to fire the glass circles. Place the 17-inch (43.2 cm) fiber-paper circle, with its arranged leaf shapes, on a kiln shelf. Center the two 16-inch (40.6 cm) glass circles on top of it; either circle can be placed on top. Fire the glass, using the Basic Fuse Schedule (see page 50).

11 When the kiln has cooled, remove the piece from it. Place the stacked 14-inch fiber-paper circles and their arranged leaf shapes on the shelf. Center the 13-inch aqua glass circles on top of them. Fire the glass, using the Basic Fuse Schedule (see page 50).

12 When the kiln has cooled, remove the piece from it. Place the layered 12-inch (30.5 cm) fiber-paper circles, with their medium leaf shape, on a kiln shelf. Center the two 11-inch (27.8 cm) glass circles on top of them; either circle can be placed on top. Fire the glass, using the Basic Fuse Schedule (see page 50).

13 If your bowl mold is new, prepare it with kiln wash and let it dry completely.

14 Use water and a plastic scrub brush to remove any fiber paper from the fused glass circles.

15 Place the 16-inch-diameter (40.6 cm) fused glass circle, which will form the fountain bowl, on the mold, textured side face down. Fire the circle, using the Basic Slump Schedule (see page 48). If the circle slumps unevenly, center it on the mold and slump it again.

Making the Supports for the Layers

16 To create the clear-glass bars that will support the fountain layers, start by cutting the 4½ x 16-inch (11.4 x 40.6 cm) clear glass into six ¾ x 16-inch (1.9 x 40.6 cm) strips. Wash and dry the strips.

17 Place the 3 x 18 inch (7.6 x 45.7 cm) strip of fiber paper on the kiln shelf, smooth side up. Stand one of the 16-inch-long (40.6 cm) dams along one edge of the paper. Line the inner surface of the dam with one of the 16-inch-long (40.6 cm) fiber-paper strips, with the paper's rough side facing the dam. Stack the clear strips on top of one another, pressing their edges up against the fiber paper. Place another 16-inch-long (40.6 cm) strip of fiber paper against the other side of the stack, with its smooth side facing the glass, and add another 16-inch-long (40.6 cm) dam. (Photo 1 on page 113 shows a similar arrangement, but the glass strips in that photo are positioned on their edges.)

18 To finish damming, position a 1 x 3-inch (2.5 x 7.6 cm) fiber-paper strip and a dam up against each end of the glass stack. Make sure all the corners are tight; then fire the glass, using the Basic Fountain-Post Fuse Schedule on page 120.

Making the Fountain-Top Leaves

19 Trace the four Fountain-Top Leaf templates (see page 125) onto four of the 3-inch (7.6 cm) fiber-paper squares. Cut out the leaf shapes, discard them, and keep the squares. Using the same templates, trace only the heart-shaped outline of each leaf onto each of four more 3-inch (7.5 cm) fiber-paper squares. Cut out these shapes, discard them, and keep the squares.

20 Place the four uncut 3-inch (7.5 cm) fiber-paper squares on the kiln shelf. Each one will serve as the base for a mold. On top of each one, place one of the squares with a cut-out leaf shape in it. Then, on top of each of these squares, place one of the squares with only a cut-out leaf outline in it. The edges of the leaves should all line up to make a multilevel mold. You now have four three-layer stacks of fiber paper.

BASIC FOUNTAIN-POST FUSE SCHEDULE

STAGE	FAHRENHEIT / CELSIUS
R1	400°F (222°C)/hour
L1	1465°F (796°C)
H1	30 minutes
R2	AFAP
L2	960°F (516°C)
H2	180 minutes
R3	16°F (9°C)/hour
L3	750°F (399°C)
H3	0 minutes
R4	32°F (18°C)/hour
L4	650°F (343°C)
H4	Off

BASIC FRIT-LEAF CAST SCHEDULE

STAGE	FAHRENHEIT / CELSIUS
R1	AFAP
L1	1465°F (796°C)
H1	20 minutes
R2	AFAP
L2	960°F (516°C)
H2	45 minutes

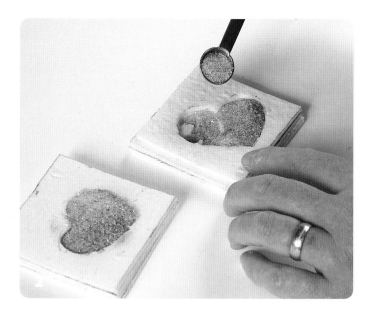

21 Fill these four leaf molds with a blend of frit colors, mounding the frit in the middle of each one (photo 2). Fire the leaves, using the Basic Frit-Leaf Cast Schedule on this page.

22 When the leaves are cool, remove them from the kiln and clean them with a plastic scrub brush and water. Remove any sharp edges with your diamond hand pads.

Drilling the Holes and Cutting the Blocks

23 To make holes for the fountain tubing, use a ⅝-inch-diameter (1.6 cm) diamond core bit to drill a hole through the center of the 14-inch (35.6 cm) fused circle and a hole through the center of the 12-inch (30.6 cm) fused circle (see Drilling Holes on pages 57–58). You may want someone to do this for you.

24 Using diamond hand pads, smooth any rough edges from the ¾ x 16-inch (1.9 x 40.6 cm) fused clear block. With the tile saw, cut this block into three 3-inch-long (7.6 cm) pieces and three 1-inch-long (2.5 cm) pieces. (You'll have a bit left over.)

Assembling the Fountain

25 Attach the tubing to the pump and place the pump and the light in the center of the fused bowl. Stand the three 3-inch (7.6 cm) glass blocks on end in the bowl (photo 3). Then thread the tubing through the hole in the 13-inch (33 cm) fused circle, textured side up, and set the circle down on the glass blocks.

26 Stand the 1-inch (2.5 cm) blocks on top of the 13-inch (33 cm) circle. Thread the tubing through the hole in the 11-inch (27.9 cm) fused circle and set that circle on the blocks. Arrange the four fountain-top leaves around the top of the tubing to camouflage it. If the tubing is too long, cut a little bit off. Fill the bowl with water.

3

Templates

HARLEQUIN CANDLE TRAY

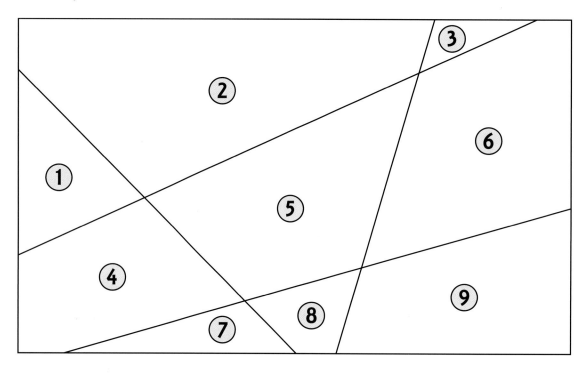

Enlarge 200%
Actual size: 7 x 12 inches (17.8 x 30.5 cm)

IRIDESCENT PENDANT

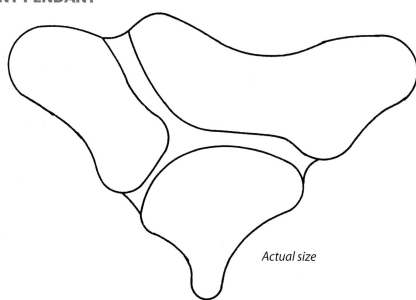

Actual size

PÂTE DE VERRE SUGAR SQUARE

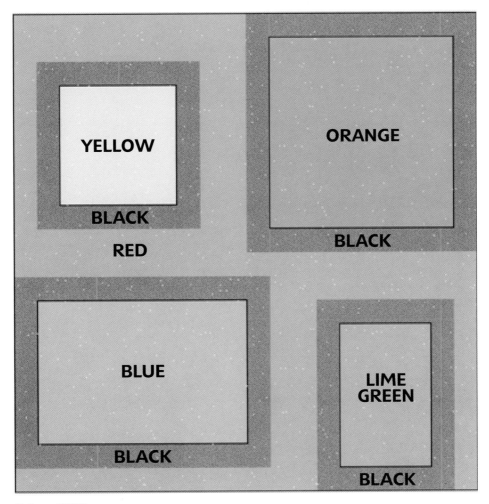

Enlarge 200%
Actual size: 10 x 10 inches (25.4 x 25.4 cm)

OPEN POCKET VASE

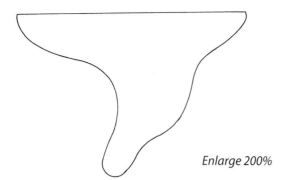

Enlarge 200%

BLUE FLAME HANGING PANEL

A = Aqua
C = Cobalt Blue
L = Light Blue
M = Midnight Blue
T = Turquoise

Enlarge 200%
Actual size: 10 x 12 inches (25.4 x 30.5 cm)

SPLIT-LEAF PHILODENRON FOUNTAIN

Enlarge 200%

Large leaf

Small leaf

Fountain-top leaves

Fountain-top leaves

Medium leaf

Acknowledgments

As with any monumental endeavor, this book was completed not through the efforts of one person, but with the support of many. Here are some of the many—and my apologies to those I may have missed mentioning during the rush to finish. This is my little Academy Awards speech, and no one gets to hold a timer.

A CAST OF TENS

My mom, Marcia Tunnock, for—well—everything

Katie Patten, for teaching me "glass" and starting me on this road in 1985

Brian Spross, for wrangling the fussy legal details

Chris Rich, my editor extraordinaire

Bart Kasden and John Widman, for their incredible photography

Bill Paley and the rest of the Glass Incarnate regulars, for their daily support during the writing process

Carol Sheppard, assistant, apprentice, right hand, for managing the photo shoot when I had to run off on a child's dental emergency

Stacy Reno, for providing play dates for Jessie and quiet writing time for me

Andrea Land, for always providing an ear for my venting and for sage advice about Getting Over It

All the artists who generously shared images of their work for publication in this book

Lize Burr and Chris Hyams, for commissioning the backsplash that led to the sushi set that led to the book contract

Curtis Awalt, for one volt to push one amp through one ohm, and other electrical wisdom

The members of Warmglass.com, who are without a doubt the most supportive and ingenious artists' community on the Internet

And finally, Boyce Lundstrom, for Glass Fusing Book One, the book that started it all for me

Brenda Griffith began kiln forming glass in the mid-1980s. The lush/stark juxtaposition and mountain colors of the Montana landscape informed her early work. In 1987 she moved to Chicago and launched Siyeh Studio (www.siyehstudio.com). The Craftsman architecture permeating the Midwest strengthened her appreciation for clean lines and infused her next stage of work with softer hues. The South's vibrant colors and saturation of light have enriched her palette and emboldened her to experiment with color and size on a much larger scale.

Sandblast etching and carving, kiln casting, pâte de verre, and other kiln-forming techniques round out her repertoire. Ms. Griffith's work is an eclectic mix of functional home furnishings (sinks, backsplashes, tiles, lighting fixtures, fountains, and vessels) and glass art (one-of-a-kind boxes, sculptures, and window and wall panels). She is a two-time NICHE Award finalist in the category "Fused Glass." Her work appears in more than 40 galleries in 20 states and Canada. Ms. Griffith teaches, mentors, and writes.

She currently resides in Atlanta with her husband, daughter, three dogs, a cat, a ferret, and four fish.

Gallery Contributors

Ellen Abbott and Mark Leva
Houston, Texas
Pages 25 and 49

Lisa Allen
Memphis, Tennessee
Page 47

Avery H. Anderson
Cheshire, Oregon
Pages 28 and 38

Diane Anderson
Park Ridge, Illinois
Pages 41 and 61

Jackie Beckman
Mesa, Arizona
Pages 58 and 62

Carol Carson
Las Vegas, Nevada
Pages 27 and 31

Geri Comstock
San Jose, California
Page 12

Karen Ehart
Tucson, Arizona
Page 10

Robin Evans
Loveland, Colorado
Page 54

Barbara Galazzo
Cold Spring, New York
Pages 57 and 58

Nancy Goodenough
Monte Rio, California
Page 19

Steve Immerman
Eau Claire, Wisconsin
Pages 14 and 21

Rick Jarvis
Bothell, Washington
Pages 30 and 33

Martin Kremer
Pound Ridge, New York
Pages 46 and 60

Richard La Londe
Freeland, Washington
Pages 45 and 51

Bob Leatherbarrow
Calgary, Alberta, Canada
Page 22

Barbara Muth
Fairfax, Virginia
Pages 36 and 40

Licha Ochoa Nicholson
Marietta, Georgia
Page 24

Lesley C.S. Nolan
Tallahassee, Florida
Pages 11 and 59

Cynthia Oliver
Salt Lake City, Utah
Pages 23 and 52

Robert Quarrick
Benicia, California
Page 56

Delores Taylor
Woodinville, Washington
Pages 15, 42, and 62

Laurel Yourkowski
Monmouth, Oregon
Page 26

William Zweifel
Elkhorn, Wisconsin
Page 35

Index